TENACITY

An Immigrant's Stories of Leadership, Navigation,
and Adaptability in
Realizing The American Dream

By
José Rolando Villarreal, J.D.

TENACITY: An Immigrant's Stories of Leadership, Navigation, and Adaptability in Realizing the American Dream

Copyright © 2020

Published by: BookBaby

Author: José Rolando Villarreal, J.D.
e-mail: TENACITYJRV@gmail.com
website: TenacityJRV.com

ISBN: 978-1-54399-701-9

Copy Editors: Rolando Villarreal, Jr., Dr. Elida G. Garza, Wyman Sanders

Cover Design and Production: Impress Printing, William Jimenez

Printed in U.S.A.

"We must go forward… but we cannot kill the past in doing so, for the past is part of our identity, and without our identity, we are nothing.

Carlos Fuentes – Mexican Novelist and Essayist - 1928-2012

"It is not the critic who counts… the credit belongs to the person who is actually in the arena, whose face is marred by dust and sweat and blood; who strives valiantly; who errs, who comes short again and again…who, at worst, if he fails, at least fails while daring greatly; so that his place shall never be with those cold and timid souls who know neither victory or defeat."

Theodore Roosevelt – U.S.A. President -1901-1909

"I am Joaquin, lost in a world of confusion, caught up in the whirl of a gringo society, confused by the rules, scorned by attitudes, suppressed by manipulation, and destroyed by modern society."

Corky Gonzales – Chicano Political Activist - 1960's

"*El respeto al derecho ajeno es la paz.*" (Respect for the rights of others is peace.)

Benito Juárez – Mexican President – 1867-1872

CONTENTS

ABOUT THE AUTHOR

José Rolando Villarreal, J.D., was born and raised in Piedras Negras, Coahuila, Mexico. At the age of eight, he immigrated to the USA in 1953, with his parents and three sisters to the border city of Eagle Pass, Texas. The Villarreal family migrated throughout several American states such as Texas, Illinois, Michigan, Indiana, Ohio, Arkansas, including some major cities, such as San Antonio, Chicago, Houston, Los Angeles, and eventually settled in San Jose, California where Villarreal graduated from San Jose State University and the University of Santa Clara Law School. He also attended numerous executive leadership courses at Harvard's John F. Kennedy School of Government.

Villarreal resides in Sanger, California with his wife. Their three sons, daughter and eight grandchildren reside nearby.

José RolandoVillarreal, J.D.

Villarreal was the Chief Public Defender for the County of Fresno for eight years and the Chief Public Defender for the County of Santa Clara for ten years. He is a former Mayor of the City of Sanger, California, former Board Chairman of the California Rural Legal Assistance Program, former adjunct professor at Fresno State University, Board Member of other numerous community organizations, and a member of the California State Bar.

ACKNOWLEDGEMENTS

I am gratefully indebted to all my family members and friends who contributed in making this book possible.

I would like to express my gratitude to my grandson, Rolando Villarreal, Jr., B.A., for his editing and for his insightfulness; to Dr. Elida G. Garza for editing and her husband, Wyman Sanders, M.Ed., for his technical assistance; Dr. Alfredo Cuéllar for his kind words in the Foreword; Judge Robert Dresser, J.D., and wife, Maria del Socorro (Choco) Leandro Dresser, M.Ed., for editing and sharing youth memories; Ramon Delgadillo, M.B.A., for his thoughtful analysis of the book; to Carlos Héctor Garza for his direct and constructive critique of the book; to my friend, Dan Ronquillo, B.A., for his insightful review of the book; to our sons, Rolando, Adrian, and Alejandro for their focus group reaction to the book; and to Meliza, our daughter, her husband, Tim, and granddaughters, Jessica and Jordan, for their evaluation of the book. Special thanks to Adrian and Meliza for their work and assistance with the illustration on the cover of the book.

Special recognition goes to my wife, Enriqueta, who contributed endless time and effort in the development of the book, especially in editing, typing, encouragement, memories, and spousal tolerance.

Thank you all.

FOREWORD

You have in your hands an autobiographical testimony of one of the millions of human beings who migrate from Mexico to the United States. His testimony describes chronologically a life that begins in Piedras Negras, Coahuila, Mexico, and ends in Sanger, California, but passes through many places: Eagle Pass, Mexico City, San Antonio, Chicago, Los Angeles, San Jose, Santa Clara, and Fresno, among others.

The author's testimony is sincere, modest, bordering on humility, instructional, with a purity tanned in the years of failures, *every defeat brings you closer to victory,* writes José Rolando Villarreal. Reading this book in many ways shows the processes with which each immigrant will identify: fear, suffering, adapting, changing, transforming, protecting, quieting, talking, risking, failing, and continuing to try the esoteric journey in the pursuit of the *American Dream.*

But while it seems like a book dedicated for those of Latin American origin, this is not the case. This is a book that should be mandatory reading for those who have not emigrated, especially for those who feel legitimate owners and heirs of this great nation, because knowing José Rolando's life, embodied in 17 chapters, will bring us closer when readers understand the vicissitudes, bitterness, challenges, impediments, envy, difficulties, needs, and urgencies of someone who refused to accept the fate of poverty, which marginalized his family.

His reading leaves us engrossed, without realizing his life's account connects hearts and souls, it seems that they are the lines that all the émigrés would like to write, and at the same time makes us weep as we notice his dedication to the family, to the just causes, to the defense of those in need. His wife describes him: *José Rolando is an anonymous hero.* Not only is he a hero, but an *inspiring* hero who says in this book what we would all want to shout, when our voices are not heard in the face of the anti-immigrant rhetoric that, like evil winds, blows in this land of justice and hopes.

In a book like this, you read the meaning of words and conclude what is not necessarily written; for example, readers testify how an emigrant becomes a model American citizen, never having lost the pride of his Mexican lineage, the love for Spanish, and the admiration of the culture of Mexico and Mexicans.

As in the sobering fables of children's stories, José Rolando finishes each chapter of his book with the *Lessons Learned*. Not a simple accomplishment to see that, from the sum of sufferings, defeats, joys, and triumphs that the author lived at every stage of his life, a wise voice rises to say *this I learned*. And the sum of what he learned makes up the philosophy of life of an emigrated, field worker, student, janitor, knife salesman, worker in the bureaucracies of the cities, finally defense lawyer, the head of government offices of lawyers who defend the indigent accused, and finally Mayor of a City in the Central Valley of California.

Impossible to forget in a foreword for this beautiful book, the importance that the author attaches to children and to teenagers. He dedicates a complete chapter to the paradigm that he and his wife Enriqueta used to raise their own family describing five basic elements rearing and educating a family. Attorney at Law José Rolando Villarreal is a champion of defending children and adolescents, many of whom ended up in front of him in the Juvenile Court, the anteroom of prisons. There José Rolando found young men and women full of rancor and anger, and with great intelligence he used that same energy that these children had to educate them on how to use it to their advantage. José Rolando says, *no minor should be arrested; sometimes his/her parents are the ones who should go to jail,* relentless and assertive he has no doubt that the behaviors that lead a minor to make mistakes and end up in front of a judge, originate from the inattention, absence of love, care, and guidance that only dedicated parents are able to achieve. *To fail children is to fail society,* José Rolando concludes.

Without a doubt, every reader will find enough reasons to love this book, for me, the synthesis of everything and the most sublime and valuable message is its title: *Tenacity.* What is life but a tenacious struggle? This book is proof of the inspiring final verses of Antonio Plaza's poem, La Voz del Inválido (*The Voice of the Disabled):*

The struggle with the world does not amaze you,
as is not a man the one that does not know how to fight,
because for fight the man was born for, as the bird was born to fly

- Dr. Alfredo Cuéllar, Former Professor at Harvard University

INTRODUCTION

American immigration life stories are basically about individuals who came or were brought to the United States out of economic necessity, hunger for better opportunities, or even worse, seeking asylum due to oppression in their country. My story is no different. While my life story reflects an unpleasantly rough, and at times severely cruel reality that most immigrants have confronted for centuries, it is also a story of resilience. It is a story about immigration, migration, navigation and adaptation to change in order to realize the American dream, by confronting and overcoming the harsh realities of life that most immigrants face in this country, sometimes barely surviving. I was *terco* (determined) to realize and live the American dream. I feel content that I realized the American dream, as I define it, while striving to be successful as a son, husband, father, grandfather, attorney, administrator, adjunct college professor, city mayor, staff training consultant, and best of all, as an American citizen.

Being an American immigrant is a state of mind, a tangle of conundrums and contradictions, but with the idea that, by culture adaptability, or even by osmosis, we as immigrants have incorporated all that constitutes the good, the happy, the sad, the bad, and the ugly as we navigate through this country, the United States of America. From being a Mexican, Mexican-American, Chicano, Latino, and Hispanic, I became an American in the most transparent and purest sense. Latinos, documented and undocumented, are no longer in a private sphere. We now have a unique identity that is quintessential American. We have become Americans proud of our Mexican heritage. My intent in writing this book is to inspire immigrants, documented and undocumented, and by extension to anyone who is related to immigrants or works with immigrants. Through the use of memoirs of leadership and cultural competence, I intend to show others how to successfully navigate the journey in the USA as immigrants. By documenting my immigrant experiences throughout this book, I believe that I am leaving a valuable legacy to my family, children, and grandchildren, and this in itself makes this effort worthwhile.

Credits and Disclaimer Regarding Lessons Learned Section

Most of the lessons learned presented in the Lessons Learned Section at the end of each chapter are in the public domain as sayings and adages. Some of the quotations presented are quotations that I have learned throughout the years by reading sources like *Quotations for Public Speakers, An Anthology* written by Robert G. Torriceli and *The Book of Power Quotes,* written by Daniel B. Baker. Some of the quotations were edited or modified by the author to reflect relevant sentiment(s).

The author gives special recognition to his wife, his parents, and all of his *abuelos, abuelas* (grandparents), *tíos* (uncles), *tías* (aunts), *padrinos* (godparents) and other *antepasados* (ancestors) who expressed the wealth of their wisdom, wit, and philosophy by manifesting their culture's personality, character, and spirit through wise and clever sayings and adages.

Definition of Terms

Mexican, Mexican-American, Chicano, Hispanic, and Latino(a)(x) are identity terms that have been used generationally through the years either by self-identification or through identification by governmental agencies. In many cases these terms are interchangeable, and can be offensive to some or a source of pride for others. The author chooses not to go into detail to identify the origin or meaning of each term, because each term has its own origin and the meaning varies depending on who is using it and with what intent it is being used. At the present time, the word Latino is being used as a universal term to include all the aforementioned terms.

CHAPTER 1

Immigration Raids - History Repeats Itself

It was a pleasant early summer morning in 1955 in the Santa Clara Valley in California, in the area now known as Silicon Valley. At the age of ten, I was living with my parents and my three sisters in San Jose for the summer as migrant workers. We had legally immigrated to the United States two years earlier, and our parents were working at one of the 36 canneries, factories where fruit was canned. My father had just come home from working the night shift and our mother was getting ready to go work the dayshift. The rest of us were staying home that day. Our family had been fortunate enough to rent a nearby small two room house in the back of a compound where the owners rented housing units to migrant families and single migrant workers. This summer day was basically a quiet working day for those that occupied all three houses in the compound.

Suddenly, we heard a commotion coming from the front of the compound. We heard and saw people yelling as they ran from the front house where some of the migrant workers lived. While we were not able to understand all that was said, we could hear someone yell, "*La Migra*" (Immigration)! Some of the migrant workers that started to run were now being pursued on foot by individuals that appeared to be armed law enforcement officers dressed in green uniforms. These officers in fact were Border Patrol Officers conducting an immigration raid. I had heard about immigration raids before, but I had not been involved in one, especially one where I or members of my family had been the victims of brutal Nazi-like tactics used by the Border Patrol.

Even though I knew that my family was in this country legally, a feeling of fear and a high degree of anxiety came over me while I stood and observed what was happening.

As I watched the group of Border Patrol Officers approaching our house, I began to realize that my family and I were in harm's way. It was quite clear to us that the Border Patrol Officers were using abusive physical brutal force to control the situation, using their large bodies to intimidate those that were thought to be their targets of detention. Some of the migrant workers were being pushed around and being yelled at, both in English and in Spanish. Apparently, the objective of the officers was to control the situation by detaining first and asking questions later.

The facial expressions of the Border Patrol Officers displayed unfeigned, violent anger and disdain, combined with a clear intent to physically cause injury to anyone who they considered to be an enemy 'alien', regardless of whether the 'alien' was documented or not documented. On the other hand, the facial expressions of the migrant workers that were being subjected to this violent raging conduct by the officers was one of real fear, anger, and anxiety. The migrant workers that I could barely see from my window were hunted down, caught, rounded up, and loaded into Border Patrol vehicles like animals and taken away to places unknown.

Our father was awakened by the commotion and reacted by yelling at us to stay inside the house. As the officers approached our house, my father tried to calm us by assuring us that everything was going to be fine and telling us that he was going to protect us. The scene sent fear through us, and we wondered how our father would be able to keep us safe, as it didn't appear he had any control over the situation. He indicated to us later that he thought that being courteous and showing the appropriate immigration documents to the officers would be sufficient compliance for the officers to leave us alone. Unfortunately, my father's efforts did not work. Our father was simply outnumbered and was given no chance of protecting anyone. The officers were on a mission and forced their way into our house without showing any identification or reason to justify their presence. How naive of us to think that the officers had to justify anything! Our mother tried to comfort us by getting us into a group hug, but she was unsuccessful, for my sisters and I were already crying in clear desperation, wishing for this terrifying experience to come to an end. In reality, the situation for my parents was just beginning to escalate to a higher degree of peril.

The officers were now in our house, pushing all of us to the ground and shouting in Spanish to our parents, asking endless questions about our immigration status, and showing no respect for any of us as human beings or allowing my parents to respond. Our father was pushed and slammed to the ground. The image of our father as a protector and defender of his family faded as I witnessed how he was overwhelmed by the officers' brutal force. I could sense that my father was more humiliated by the fact that all this savagery was being carried out in front of his family. His face expressed a sense of loss of dignity as a human being. My mother, who always provided support to my father and protected us, was clearly restricted by the circumstances, but not totally so. She was now furiously screaming and was somehow allowed to retrieve the demanded immigration documents while my father continued being pinned down to the floor. The officers briefly perused the documents and immediately returned them to my mother. The intruding officers left the house just as they had entered it - without uttering a word of explanation, apology, or remorse.

What these Border Patrol Officers left behind were lifelong emotional scars that remain in my mind to this day. This horrific incident destroyed any belief that I and my family were welcomed in this country legally or otherwise. It has taken a long time for me to cope effectively with the dehumanizing and traumatic effect of the mean spirited and cowardly actions by these Border Patrol Officers. As a matter of fact, I had forgotten the specifics of this incident until just recently, when I began to narrate the specific details of this story. The trauma that my family and I endured that day was buried deep in my mind and it all begin to come back to me along with the same degree of pain as we experienced that day.

Years after the incident, I found out that this and many other similar immigration raids were part of what was a formally documented government deportation program referred to as Operation Wetback, a well-planned and well-executed program initiated under the administration of President Eisenhower in 1954. Eventually, more than two million Mexicans, including thousands that were or had already become American citizens, were deported to Mexico under this program.

History repeats itself. What we as Mexicans, Americans of Mexican descent, and other immigrants who are experiencing the same treatment today is not new. The names of these programs may change but the anti-immigrant sentiment remains. We must recognize this for what it is - conduct unbecoming of a country that refers to itself as a nation that welcomes immigrants. American anti-immigration sentiment is one of the biggest obstacles or walls that immigrants must overcome. We must do everything possible to successfully navigate our way through the immigration labyrinth in front of us, no matter how challenging the obstructions placed in our path are, in order to reach the American Dream, however we define that dream.

LESSON LEARNED

- "You gain strength, courage, and confidence by every experience in which you really stop to look fear in the face. You are able to say to yourself, "I lived through this horror. I can take the next thing that comes along."

Eleanor Roosevelt –
First Lady of the United States – 1933-1945

CHAPTER 2

Searching for My Cultural Roots

As a child growing up in the northern part of Mexico, I listened to my mother talking about our family living in Mexico City in the late 1940's. We lived in an area of the city called Tlatelolco, in a building that she referred to as *la aduana* (federal customs building). My mother described the building as an enormously beautiful two-story building that was made of stone. The tall walls of the building enclosed a patio with gardens and a large fountain in the center. As a six or seven-year-old, I got excited every time my mother talked about having lived in that building.

Plaza de Tres Culturas 1979: My wife and I on our first trip to Mexico City in search of the aduana, the building I lived in as a child. We did not find it on this trip.

Recently, my wife and I visited Mexico City and found the building in Tlatelolco. Mother was right. The seemingly ancient building is not only beautiful but boasts a fascinating history on the development of Mexico and the Mexican people. It is located in the center of Tlatelolco known as *La Plaza de Tres Culturas.*

In the book entitled *Distant Neighbors-a Portrait of the Mexicans,* the author, Alan Riding, writes about the Tlatelolco area in this manner:

"Amidst the noise and fumes of Mexico City, there is a quiet square where the modern Foreign Ministry building and a sixteenth-century Spanish Colonial church looks onto the remains of the pre-Hispanic pyramids of Tlatelolco. The government has named it the Plaza of Three Cultures to venerate Mexico's mixed-blood heritage or *mestizaje.* In front of the church, a plaque carries these simple but moving words: "On August 13, 1521, heroically defended by Cuauhtémoc, Tlatelolco fell into the hands of Hernán Cortés. It was neither a triumph nor a defeat: it was the painful birth of the *mestizo* nation that is Mexico today.""

Plaza de las Tres Culturas - Foto: Jorge Pablo de Aquínaco - Post Art De Mexico S.A. de C.V., Calle 33 No.484 entre 42 y 46 Fracc. G.G., Merida, Yucatan, C.P. 97118 MEXICO

The building my mother described is part of the church complex in the *Plaza de Tres Culturas.* The Spaniards built the church and building with stones removed from the pyramids they destroyed. In the sixteenth century, this building originally housed a convent and in later years was used as a warehouse, a prison, a customs house, and recently became part of a larger museum that is now open to the public. This allowed me to walk into the patio where I used to live and play as a two-year old child and appreciate the beauty and historical significance of the building my mother used to talk to me about.

Only once in its history was this building occupied as a private residence (1945-1948). It was during this period of time that our family lived there with two other families, one of which was the family of my Uncle Ramiro Ramírez and Aunt Amparo Pérez Ramírez along with their first three children. Our two families occupied all the second floor. My uncle worked as the Administrative Secretary to the Director of Federal Customs in the administrative offices housed in *la aduana*. The Director of Customs happened to be the brother of former Mexican President Lázaro Cárdenas. To think that I actually lived in such a place is fascinating. The other persons that also lived there were the groundskeeper and his family. They lived on the first floor where the customs offices were also located.

Tío Ramiro and Tía Amparo Ramírez and their children. (1954)

This building was not only part of Tlatelolco, an Aztec sister city of Tenochtitlan (downtown Mexico City) in the early 1300's, but was also the site of the last battle that the Aztecas (Mexicas) fought against the Spanish Conquistadores in 1521, thus becoming the grounds where Mexico, the nation, was born. This building was also used as a prison during the Mexican Revolution (1910-1920). It is said that Pancho Villa, the legendary Mexican revolutionary, was incarcerated in this same building complex for a year or so.

The *Plaza de Tres Culturas* was also the site where the now infamous 1968 pre-Mexico City Olympics massacre took place when more than 300 student demonstrators were killed ten days before the Olympics. Today, this building is part of a museum that venerates the pre-Colombian, the Spanish Colonial, and the modern epochs of Mexican history. Excavations are still being conducted at the pyramid portion of the site.

The relative significance of my recent visit to the *Plaza de Tres Culturas* in Mexico City is the valuable emotional affinity that I felt towards Mexico upon setting foot on this historical, almost sacred, birth site of modern Mexico, a country full of rich cultural history. I actually felt goosebumps as I stood there in this particular location in Mexico, the country where I was born, and the land that my family eventually left for the same basic reason that most other American immigrants had left their homeland – economic necessity.

It was October 1953 when our family permanently crossed the border to the north. Immigrating to the United States of America was an event that would forever change my life. I, along with my parents and three sisters, would join millions of immigrants to this land of opportunity that we know as *Los Estados Unidos*, The United States of America (USA).

LESSON LEARNED

- In order to understand the value of the present, we must understand the value of the past.

CHAPTER 3

Remembering the Border Town of Piedras Negras

My parents, José María and Elisa, my sisters María del Socorro, Lidia Elisa, Tomasita, and I were all born in the Mexican border city of Piedras Negras, in the State of Coahuila, Mexico. Piedras Negras was founded in 1849 as a military post, prompted by the American border side military establishment of Fort Duncan (later Eagle Pass, Texas) in 1849 as a protective measure against the Native Americans (Apaches). Piedras Negras (Black Rocks) was so named for the coal deposits in the local area. It became a prosperous city due to coal mining and was subsequently elevated from a *villa* (village) to a *ciudad* (city). In 1888, the city was named Ciudad Porfirio Díaz, in honor of then President of Mexico, Porfirio Díaz. The name was said to have been changed back to Piedras Negras after the 1911 political uprising that resulted in the Mexican Revolution. Piedras Negras continued to prosper after the years of the Revolution due to the economic connection the city provided between the United States and Mexico; coal mining, railroad, and political evolvement were large factors in the city's proliferation. But just as Piedras Negras had its economic prosperity, it also had its problems that affected economically strapped families who were barely making ends meet. It was under this setting that I was born. Recently I was told by my mother that my father was living and working in the USA as an undocumented worker when I was born. The only reason why my father was working in the USA was the almost universal reason - economic necessity.

I remember Piedras Negras as a vibrant Mexican city where its residents were constantly moving in the early hours of the day, engaging in daily activities with an attitude full of vigor. My family was economically poor but we as children hardly knew it.

In the early 1950's, a typical day in *Piedras* (as we used to call Piedras Negras) would start with street vendors loudly selling milk, firewood, sweet bread, tamales, ice (in the summer), and many other house goods. The downtown main streets of Zaragoza and Allende were bustling with cars and horse buggy taxis transporting USA tourists. The block long enclosed *Mercado Zaragoza* (marketplace with many vendors) was the place to buy and sell daily fresh meat, fruits and vegetables, as well as clothing and other items such as Mexican artisan souvenirs. Workers in restaurants and nightclubs such as La Fortuna, El México Moderno, Las Trancas, El Golfito, Las Cabañitas, El Club Victoria, El Campestre, and Terraza América were getting ready for the daily business of offering traditional Mexican dishes and entertainment. *La Plaza de Armas* (the main plaza), *La Catedral*, (the main church), and *La Presidencia* (the Civic Presidential Building) were all located next to the international bridge by which the two countries were connected. The main plaza area drew the usual crowds from the *colonias* (neighborhoods) such as El Mundo Nuevo, La Gonzalez, La Colonia Americana, and many others. Movie theaters like El Cinelandia, El Rodriguez, and El Teatro Acuña were setting up for movie presentations. Sundays were typical. Devout Catholics greeted the early morning sun by attending mass. Midday Sunday activities included a trip to La Villa de Fuente, known as La Villita, for a *día de campo* (picnic) by the Río Escondido. Sunday nights consisted of a family walk at the main plaza where vendors sold *paletas* (ice cream bars), gardenias, and *suegras* (sling shot toys). Young ladies and young men would walk in a pathway within the plaza in an opposite circular way in order to face each other in a ritual of courting and socializing with members of the opposite sex, while mothers, fathers, older brothers, and grandmothers of the young ladies kept a watchful eye from a distance to ensure respect for the young maidens. Sunday nights were always festive, full of social activities that included conversation, music, dance, and food shared with family and friends.

The dark side of Piedras reared its ugly head in *cantinas* (bar saloons). *La Zona Roja* (zone of tolerance) was wrought with *ficheras* (ladies of the night), practicing the oldest profession in the world.

Special occasions, such as *fiestas* (festivals), public events, carnivals, and parades displayed all the joy in Piedras Negras in the early 1950's, boosting the citizens' spirits. What would liven up the spirit of *Piedras* the most was the festive attitude of the resident population. Although stratified by class, the *Nigropetenses* (residents of Piedras Negras) found common ground in working and celebrating life together. Whether it was through sporting events, festivals, dances, or flooding disasters, the residents of *Piedras* always showed unity.

Piedras Negras had its local unique characters that roamed the streets of the city as free spirits. I remember Lolo, a mentally ill individual, who was always singing, talking to himself, or acting belligerent, but never harming anyone. I also remember Cuco walking the streets wearing a number of hats at the same time, and Pacitos who literally walked taking little steps at a time. All these mentally ill characters were certainly reflective of a local cultural fabric that included true diversity and tolerance. And then there was Chalío, the local street clown, who brought joy and laughter to both children and parents at street corners, while trying to sell a product as part of the act.

I also remember watching a public funeral in which thousands of residents lined the streets of Piedras Negras to pay tribute to a local young man known as *El Sabio* (The Wise One). He was so smart as a young student that at times he substituted for his professor at the local school. *El Sabio* joined the American military service as a volunteer to fight in the Korean war. The practice of Mexican citizens volunteering for military service in the USA was not as common then as it is today. *El Sabio* had been promised citizenship by the USA upon finishing his tour of military service. Unfortunately, he was killed in combat. He was buried in Piedras Negras with all USA military honors, including draping his casket with the American flag.

Lastly, there was Doña Virginia, who lived in our neighborhood, and was known as a *curandera* (healer), a *bruja* (witch), and a fortune teller, all rolled into one. Doña Virginia was the aunt and guardian of three kids that my cousins and I played with daily. She lived next door to the house where our family lived with our grandmother.

Doña Virginia was a stern looking lady, and I describe her as such because, although she was always gentle and polite to us, she was somewhat cruel and abusive with her nephews. Doña Virginia was truly a clever business woman who provided business services in a variety of areas. She had clients that came from far-away places to consult with her regarding their fortune, their future, their health, and the health of others. Doña Virginia used a traditional Spanish deck of cards and provided a decorative environment to give flavor to the service of fortune telling. Doña Virginia cured the young and the elderly through the use of folk pagan medicine, including plants and *oraciones* (prayers). We always knew when Doña Virginia was 'curing' someone because of the strong smell of rotten eggs that permeated the entire house. We would gladly go outside to play. Doña Virginia was also involved in *brujeria* (witchcraft) for the good or bad of whoever requested the service, for a reasonable fee, of course. Certain rooms of Doña Virginia's house were decorated appropriately with tools of the profession, such as plants, cards, embalmed owls and dead cats. This was not the scary part. The scary part was at nighttime when Doña Virginia decided that it was time for us visitors to go home. She suggested that it was time for a *cuentito* (a short story), that she told us, in essence, to kick us out of her home. But because she wanted to appear to be nice and kind to us, she made up or used her repetitive stories of *la bruja* (the witch). Although we were fascinated by the stories, by the end of ten minutes or so, the *bruja* tale was so scary that we pleaded with her to stop telling it as we started to run to our house.

Doña Virginia was a character that certainly reflected a fascinating cultural aspect of Piedras Negras in the early 1950's. As destiny would have it, about a year after we crossed to the USA, the big flood of June 1954 devastated Piedras Negras and the house where Doña Virginia lived. We never saw nor heard of her or her nephews again.

On the family front, my father soon became politically involved in Piedras Negras and consequently was appointed to be *alcaide* (warden) in charge of the local jail. During his tenure as the warden, his leadership abilities were challenged, resulting in the escape of three prisoners. Although this happened at night when he was home sleeping during off duty hours, my father was incarcerated on charges of criminal misconduct. Back then, you could be incarcerated without a hearing or trial and without bail for months.

Since my father was the only wage earner in our family, his six months stay in jail seemed like an eternity for my mother and us kids. My mother fed us and paid the rent by sewing for others, and making and selling tamales. A handful of relatives brought food over for us. Needless to say, it was a very difficult and challenging time for our family, even though we got to visit my father in jail on a weekly basis. I remember that as Christmas Eve was approaching, my mother and some other relatives, who were very involved in the church, went and asked the priest to ask for permission from the local jail authorities to allow my father to spend Christmas Eve with us. Permission was granted and my father returned back to jail on Christmas Day. Finally, after six months, my *Tío* Ramiro posted bail on behalf of my father and the charges against my father were dropped soon thereafter. Enough said about criminal justice in the Mexico of the 1950's.

After this tragic incident, our family moved to neighboring Ciudad Acuña, Coahuila, where I was enrolled in second grade at the local school. Unable to find work in Ciudad Acuña, my father immigrated alone as an undocumented worker to the United States where he easily found work as a butcher in Chicago. Many of the difficulties and obstacles that people faced then and today in crossing the border never precluded my father's access to the USA and finding work to provide for his family. After a few months of living alone with her children in Ciudad Acuña, my mother moved us back to Piedras Negras to our grandmother's home where my mother took care of us while my father was gone.

While we lived in Piedras Negras, we ran and played throughout the streets, we went fishing in the nearby *Río Bravo* river (the Rio Grande River), and we enjoyed the carnivals that came to town from time to time. We also snuck into *las carpas* (tent theaters) to watch performances. It was not uncommon for traveling theaters to be in town for a week or two, and though the entertainment we enjoyed was primitive compared to today's standards, to us it was just as enjoyable. Traveling carnivals, for example, were not mechanized yet. Instead, the carnival operators hired children such as ourselves to get on top of circular platforms to physically push *las sillas voladoras* (flying chairs) to provide entertainment for paying customers. Instead of monetary payment, we were paid with coupons that we used to enter the carnival and ride the attractions for free. The kids that were poor, such as ourselves, were the ones working for what we considered to be the higher-class population of kids who enjoyed these rides without having to do unpaid manual labor. As children, we did not think of it in those adult terms. We were just enjoying life. As a matter of fact, at the time we were not even aware that we were economically poor. We had food, shelter, a mother, a father and an extended family. This was sufficient for us.

My experiences in elementary school in Mexico were generally very positive, sprinkled with some negative experiences. Due to the student socio-economic diversity in the school in Piedras Negras, half of the kids in the class attended school well-fed, well-clothed, and comfortable, while the other half attended class barefoot and hungry. This dichotomy would sometimes cause a level of bitterness/anger that showed up when these children of poverty bullied other students. Many times, I was placed in situations during my elementary school years in which the kids who lived in extreme poverty physically threatened me in order to obtain my lunch money or my lunch. I was a small child, skinny, short, and otherwise unthreatening. Consequently, there were many physical fights where I ended up on the losing side trying to protect my lunch or my lunch money.

On the other hand, students that came from well-to-do families flaunted their economic status with disdain towards the students that were not well-to-do. On one occasion, as I was planning to participate in my first-grade graduation ceremony, I faced a dilemma. The school was determined to enforce a policy of having all graduating students wear a military type school uniform that included a jacket that my parents could not afford to buy. My resourceful mother was able to borrow the required military jacket from a well-to-do friend whose son had graduated the year before. Unfortunately, the son and I did not get along and on the day of the graduation ceremony, the boy decided that he wanted his jacket back and was determined to get it back from me, by force if necessary. Since I was equally as determined to wear the jacket during the ceremony, the conflict regarding the jacket was not resolved peacefully. I literally had to hide from the boy until the commencement of the ceremony. After the ceremony, as I was returning the jacket to the rightful owner, the boy, both of us engaged in a physical altercation that ended in a bloody draw that I would remember for the rest of my life. On the positive side of all of this,

I learned how to navigate through unwelcoming and hostile environments, although it cost me some beatings and sometimes even my lunch.

My first-grade graduation with the borrowed jacket.

During the 1950's, throughout the community of Piedras Negras, there was a high value placed on your first six years of education. After the sixth grade, those whose family was well off continued on toward a higher education, while those whose family could not afford the raised fees of schooling dropped out to go to work wherever they could to help their ever economically strapped families. Economic times were not good for dirt poor families in Piedras Negras during the 1950's. This harsh reality clearly influenced my parents in deciding to immigrate to the United States of America.

Happy Days in La Villita

In 1953, soon after being back in Piedras Negras for a third time, my father and our family moved to a tiny nearby community known as *La Villita* (a village), literally a town with a population of about 1,000 that had a river, Río Escondido, running through the town. La Villita was a typical Mexican village town with a church, a school, and a central area that was referred to as *La Plaza Principal* (the main plaza). As young children, we headed to the plaza unaccompanied by our parents. We spent many hours at a time, playing with friends, with no preoccupations of danger whatsoever. The family structure during the time period in the early 1950's was a more or less relaxed one, where parents were confident that their children were safe, with little emphasis being placed on protection of children. Unlike many children of today, we enjoyed our freedom to its maximum potential as young children. As I remember, these years of my life were spent happily, rich in joyful moments with no desire of materialistic possessions. From time to time, we would go to *al otro lado* (the other side) in the United States. Ironically, for the kids that lived in Piedras Negras, *el otro lado* meant Eagle Pass, Texas, whereas for the kids who resided in Eagle Pass, *el otro lado* meant Piedras Negras, Coahuila, Mexico.

Like other homes where we previously lived, the house where we lived in *La Villita* did not have electricity, plumbing, or running water, only a water well outside. The lack of these basic necessities did not stop me from enjoying life in this little town. Nonetheless, we needed to find ways of making money. I recall an early entrepreneurship experience at the age of eight. Casimiro, a friend of mine, owned a donkey that we nicknamed *la burra de Casimiro* (Casimiro's donkey). Because we lived close to a border town, we would see many *Norte Americanos* (North American) tourists who would pass by in convoys of recreational vehicles and aluminum covered trailers. One day, it occurred to me to suggest to my friend Casimiro to escort his donkey to the bridge on the river with the objective of encouraging tourists to stop so they could take pictures of us with the donkey by the side of the road. Casimiro thought this to be a great idea too, and we began taking the donkey across the bridge in an attempt to set our stereotypical Mexican appearance as a business venture. After the tourists had taken pictures of us with the donkey, the tourists usually rewarded us with an American dime or quarter, which was a lot of money to us at that time. Culturally, the Americans tourists saw us as a tourist attraction. From their perspective, we typified a piece of the Mexican cultural fabric. The American tourists probably assumed that Mexicans looked, dressed, and acted the same way throughout all Mexico. Nevertheless, Casimiro and I considered this photo-op process as a business venture, smiling and posing, collecting money very graciously, and moving on to our next clients. As a side venture, we sometimes picked pecans from the local pecan trees and sold them to the American tourists or to individuals who used the pecan nuts to make candy. As I recall, my friend Casimiro and I enjoyed every moment of these experiences. The pictures of Casimiro, the donkey, and I most likely appeared in magazines such as National Geographic.

I remember taking part in many cultural traditional practices, especially those practices that took place when someone died. In *La Villita,* just as in other Mexican communities, it was customary for funeral services to begin in the home of the deceased with a *velorio* (a wake) usually for a day or two followed by the funeral. On the evening after the funeral a *novena* (nine-day series of *rosarios* (rosaries), on behalf of the departed, was started. At the *velorio* and the *rosarios*, people would bring food and coffee, known as *café de olla* (coffee brewed in a clay pot with cinnamon) and *café con leche* (coffee with milk). The mood at the *velorios* was always festive. Mourners were merry as they celebrated the life of the departed. The body of the deceased was present in the house and people gathered around it to pay their respects. During this time, relatives and friends eulogized the departed using a macabre sense of humor to tell stories and jokes to illustrate the impact that the life of the departed had on them. I remember these funeral events as joyful moments, despite their morbid nature and the loss of loved ones. By the way, the *café de olla* and the *café con leche* were always delicious!

This is how I remember Piedras Negras.

LESSON LEARNED

- There is nothing more beneficial to your life than the memories that are preserved from your childhood. Sometimes, these memories are the best education that you can get.

CHAPTER 4

First Year in the USA - Life Changing Experiences

On October 21, 1953, my father managed to acquire all the legal documents necessary for all our family members to become permanent residents of the United States of America. On that same day, our family left Mexico, successfully immigrating with nothing else but two pieces of luggage and six hearts full of hope. We crossed the Rio Grande River to spend the evening at my aunt's house in Eagle Pass, Texas with plans to leave to San Antonio, Texas late that night. My father arranged with a friend that owned a produce truck to take us to San Antonio, 150 miles away. Close to midnight, my father's friend came by and away we went to San Antonio. As an eight-year old child, I did not want to leave and move to the USA. La Villita represented all of the things I did not want to leave behind. I was extremely happy there, and although I tried to understand the reasoning behind moving to a new country, I still remember looking back on the beautiful Mexican countryside and looking down at the road racing underneath me, silently saying goodbye to La Villita and Piedras Negras, the places where I had spent so many happy moments.

Our family's legal immigration document (passport) for permanent residence in the USA

Hello, San Antonio

On October 22, 1953, at about three o'clock in the morning, we arrived at a produce distribution center parking lot right in the center of downtown San Antonio. Mi Tierra Cafe (now known as Mi Tierra Cafe and Bakery) was located right in the middle of the produce parking lot now known as the Market Square. After having spent a three-hour long trip in the back of a windowless produce truck along with many crates full of fruits and vegetables, my parents, my sisters, and I were ready to get out, stretch, and see what was waiting for us in this new country.

As we got off the truck, there stood before us a gigantic building about thirty to forty stories high (presently known as the Tower Life Building) that was brightly illuminated in a dark San Antonio night. Amazed as any

19

eight-year old boy could be, I laid my eyes upon this edifice and I was forever changed. The image of this building became my first impression of the United States of America.

Tower Life Building in San Antonio, Texas

I did not remember seeing a building as awe-inspiring prior to this moment. The effect was so profound that, every time I go back to San Antonio, I return to this particular site to relive the significance of that moment in my life. The lights on the building still resonate feelings of astonishment, transformation, and transcendence within me. In essence, this lighted building became, at best, a beacon of hope, and at worst, a warning of traumatic change to come.

Today, my wife and I visit Mi Tierra Cafe every time we go to San Antonio to meet with family and friends. The food is great, the ambiance is joyful, and service is awesome. We make it a point to go there when we arrive and before we leave San Antonio, plus several times in between. One time we had the pleasure of meeting the eldest son Jorge Cortez, (present owner/manager) of the original owner and he told us the story of how his parents came to this country as immigrants and later converted the original little restaurant into the 24 hour - 7 days a week, 600 employee business that it is today.

My mother and I with family at Mi Tierra Cafe.

Reverting back to that October morning in 1953, my father contacted a cousin of his who lived in San Antonio. Within a few days of us living with my father's cousin, my father found a job working as a laborer in a pecan candy factory just outside of downtown San Antonio. Consequently, we moved to a tiny apartment in an area known as Westside San Antonio where recently arrived Mexican immigrant families lived. Little did I know that for the next ten years or so, our family would end up living in the barrio section of every American city in which we, as a family, would reside. The list of these American cities included San Antonio, Chicago, Houston, San Jose, and Los Angeles.

Within a few days after moving to Westside San Antonio, my mother enrolled my three sisters and me in Navarro Elementary School, named after José Antonio Navarro, a signer of the Texas Declaration of Independence in 1836. Although the school was located within a Mexican barrio, we as Mexican kids were expected to learn the English language fairly rapidly. These expectations made it a challenge for us to switch from a basically monolingual speaking cultural environment to a bilingual speaking cultural environment.

Navarro School, in San Antonio, Texas, the first school I attended in the USA.

Life in San Antonio was fairly routine and pleasant. My father was earning enough money to provide for the family, my mother was content carrying out her spousal responsibilities, and we were happy attending school and making new friends.

Although I was too young to really appreciate it, I remember San Antonio as being a great city. With its rich cultural mix of Mexican, German, and Anglo-Saxon heritage, San Antonio was and still is a city of cultural tolerance, at least at the macro social, economic and political levels. It has the downtown area, the Market Square, the annual cultural festivals, and the restaurants. Unfortunately, I also remember San Antonio for the residual aspects of cultural divisions and extreme poverty.

As an eight-year old student, I started to notice how differently the Anglo-Saxon school teachers and *Tejano* children (those born in Texas who spoke Spanglish or Tex-Mex— a mix of Spanish and English) were behaving towards me. It was clear to me that the fact that I was from Mexico and did not speak English was a major factor that resulted in the attitude that was being projected toward me. It was hard to believe that this was happening in the barrio. Both teachers and students were surprisingly unwelcoming. My response options were limited.

In attempting to blend into my surroundings, I fell into a catch twenty-two situation. If I spoke Spanish, I would be castigated by the teacher. On the other hand, if I tried to speak English, I would be the subject of ridicule by the *Tejano* children, and I knew I didn't need any more harassment from the children. The daily language challenges at school forced me to adapt faster because, as my mother used to say: *"Tienes que aprender a hablar íngles porque una persona bilingüe vale por dos"* ("You have to learn how to speak English because a bilingual person is worth twice as much"). In the long run, I realized that my mother was right but my self-confidence took a nose dive in the process.

As I proceeded to confront my inner personal conflict, I realized that this struggle to adapt in San Antonio was not necessarily a walk in the park, but was soluble. After a relatively happy but brief stay of several months in the beautiful city of San Antonio, my parents told us that we were leaving San Antonio and moving on to the city of Chicago.

Following what became a set pattern of economic migrant thinking, my father decided to move to Chicago based on a conversation that he had with a cousin that was passing by San Antonio on his way back to Chicago where he lived. As a result of this conversation, my father was convinced that our family would be better off economically in Chicago and since his cousin was offering to take us in his car, we would be wise to take advantage of the opportunity.

I was certainly sad to leave San Antonio but I had no choice in the matter. We were on our way to Chicago, seeking and hopefully finding a better life. At that stage in my life I really had no idea what a better life would be like, but when my father said "*Vamonos*" ("Let's go"), it was time to move with no questions asked. In 1953, a couple of days before New Year's Eve, we were on our way to the great city of Chicago, Illinois.

Hello, Chicago

When we arrived in Chicago on New Year's Day of 1954, the city was engulfed by a ferocious snowstorm that had been furiously hitting the area for days. What was astonishing to me was how people were seemingly going about their daily business as if it were any other normal day. I later learned that these extreme snowstorms were very common in Chicago. In other words, for Chicagoans, this day had been just another normal day. The weather set the tone for what would become one of the biggest adaptation challenges of my life.

We ended up in a Chicago neighborhood in which no one spoke or understood Spanish. My father's cousin introduced my father to a friend who took our family in when we arrived in Chicago. The host family lived in a very small house, barely big enough to accommodate their own family. Upon arriving, it was clear to me that the host family had not been expecting us. However, everyone in the host family was Spanish-speaking and made us feel welcome from the moment we arrived; even though we slept in the attached garage, they graciously allowed us full use of their small home.

I remember several members of the host family watching football on television all day and I began to wonder why they would take the time for such an abnormal daily routine. Later, I learned that on New Year's Day, it was customary for American football fans to watch College Bowl games all day long. Talk about culture shock. Looking back, I now believe that this host Mexican family was in the process of acculturating to the American way of life.

The snowstorm hitting Chicago continued for a few days and forced us to stay crammed inside the small house, a situation that was starting to become unpleasant for both the host family and our family. We weren't used to this type of harsh weather in Mexico, but then again, we were not used to the many new things that were coming at us. I was amazed to see how well the host family had adapted to the severely cold weather in this part of the world.

Luckily, my father found a job in a meat market (he was a butcher by trade) right away and we were able to move to a tiny two room basement apartment. This basement apartment was in a three-story apartment building. Due to the unpleasant weather outside, it was challenging for my mother to keep us kids busy and entertained inside this tiny apartment, while my father was at work all day. The basement had no windows. We had a single light bulb hanging from the middle of the hallway and it was on all day long. I remember my father coming home from work exhausted and just wanting to lay down and rest for a little while, as my mother tried to keep us quiet as he rested. The Chicago cold weather also took a toll on him, and due to lack of transportation, he had to commute by bus or walk to and from work.

School Days in Chicago

Within a few days of arriving in Chicago, my three sisters and I were enrolled in a nearby elementary school. It turned out that we were now living in a Polish refugee poverty-stricken area of Chicago where the local school system focused on educating predominately Polish refugee children.

My initial experience with being enrolled in a Chicago education system was an incident that occurred on one of my first days of school. I entered the classroom and was immediately placed in a back corner of the classroom because I did not speak or understand English. Every day, my teacher, a middle-aged Anglo-Saxon woman, continued placing me in the back corner of the room, with no effort on her part to communicate with me or to integrate me into the class.

One day a student in the class lost some money, and I was immediately accused of stealing it. The teacher searched me in front of all the class and found some change in my pocket that my mother had given me for lunch. Without asking any questions, or giving me a chance to explain, the teacher took the money and sent me to the principal's office. Again, no school staff member spoke Spanish and I was totally unsuccessful in trying to explain that the money in question was lunch money that my mother had given me that morning and that I was not even physically close enough to anyone to have taken anything from anyone. I was expecting to have my situation recognized by school officials as unfairly hurtful to me, but nothing happened. I was lost, constantly asking myself why this unfair action was being taken against me.

The teacher indicated to me somehow that she wanted me to continue in the back of the class room looking at books instead of bothering her with my distractions due to my language deficiencies. Thankfully, the Polish refugee kids were somewhat more receptive to me, making small but significant efforts to smile and speak to me.

Eventually, after six weeks of trying to deal with this completely incomprehensible situation, I spoke to my parents about my demoralizing experience. I explained to them that I was not learning anything by just looking at books and pleaded with them to do something. My parents had very limited options in trying to resolve the problem and within a week of having heard my story of horrid segregation, decided to move the family to the southwestern part of Chicago where large populations of Mexicans and Italians lived.

My parents hoped that the staff of the schools in that part of the city would be more sensitive to the educational needs of a Mexican kid like myself. My parents did not question what was happening in the first school; they just basically said to me, "*Ignora lo negativo, demuestra respeto, y sigue adelante*" ("Ignore the negative, show respect, and move on"). My parents may not have known how to speak the English language, but they were wise enough to confront this challenge successfully by moving away to another part of town.

As a result of the move, I did better in the school system of Westside Chicago. Although the school did not have an organized bilingual program, the school staff had sufficient bilingual ability to communicate in order to help me learn the English language. The first word in English that I truly felt comfortable learning and using was the word 'maybe'. I had learned to use 'yes' or 'no.' but I suffered consequences by using such definitive vocabulary. The word 'maybe' allowed me the flexibility to avoid those consequences. As I continued to face this new world, I began to recognize my parents' ability to adapt to change, a change that was ironically constant.

In order to help out with family finances, I began selling Spanish newspapers after school in nearby downtown Chicago. The newspaper, El Semanal, was a weekly bilingual Spanish/English newspaper that I bought for three cents and sold for five cents, with a profit of two cents per paper. I was trying to help my family in any way I could because my father's salary as a butcher was not sufficient to make ends meet. I realize now that possibly the reason why I was able to sell all the newspapers that I set out to sell was that the buyers were actually buying the paper because they felt sorry for a nine-year old boy hustling in busy downtown Chicago. For whatever reason, I felt very good coming home with nickels and dimes after successfully selling all the newspapers.

We moved to a storefront in an abandoned building that previously was used to house stores and business offices. The cross streets that I recall crossing in this somewhat desolate area were Halsted and Polk Avenues, close to famous historic Maxwell Street. Years later I found out that, in 1954, these business areas and the surrounding housing areas had been declared to be blighted areas and were part of a long-term urban renewal plan where the future University of Illinois at Chicago was going to be built.

In our rented storefront, my parents improvised by dividing the store area by hanging bed sheets to create rooms. I remember how antiquated the brick buildings looked. These dusty old multi-story empty buildings attracted the criminally-active adolescents who had the propensity of causing trouble in dangerous and disruptive ways. As a child, I enjoyed our living quarters because the abandoned buildings made for a great playground in the daytime. My friends and I ran and hid throughout the abandoned empty buildings, enjoying the somewhat weirdly attractive aspect of such a desolate area.

The streets of nearby downtown Chicago were not attractive to me and were, in many ways, much more dangerous than the streets where we lived. As a boy moving throughout downtown Chicago or playing throughout our neighborhood, I witnessed many violent events that included violent altercations that led to stabbings. These incidents terrified me, but due to a code of silence within myself, I did not say anything to anybody, including my parents.

The fact that I was new in the city, coupled with not knowing the language, scared me even more. I was always scanning for situations that could potentially place me in harm's way. On one occasion, I witnessed a robbery assault. I ran away and hid from any sort of involvement, not being able to explain it to anyone or to seek help. I was so frightened that I could not utter a word for several minutes. What I saw on these streets was extremely different from what I had seen in San Antonio or even in Mexico. This was a part of America that I did not like.

Chicago had all kinds of people. Unfortunately, that included unsavory people as well. The extreme violent nature of the robbery that I witnessed showed me that human beings had the capacity of being cruel and vicious savages, stealing and killing for personal gain.

On another occasion, I came upon a dead body. The body was abandoned, fully exposed, lying in a limp, awkward position devoid of any human dignity and starting to decompose. The body was lying in one of the abandoned buildings in an open area, next to a big building entrance. Upon seeing the body, I simply ran, hoping that I would not be seen or victimized. Thereafter, every time I passed by that particular building, I was reminded of the body that left me with an eerie, disturbing, and unforgettable feeling which I always associated with this particular neighborhood.

The other thing that I will never forget is how cold Chicago was in early 1954. Despite my mother's valiant efforts to clothe us properly and finding refuge in warm places such as churches during windy snow storms, the Chicago cold was always victorious in traumatizing us as children. I have never returned to Chicago but hope to someday.

Hello, Michigan

In the meantime, my father was once again considering the idea of moving out of Chicago to another city or even another state. Having talked to a family member and a friend, my father was again convinced that the working opportunities were better in the state of Michigan, where the farm workers were supposedly economically better off than poor folks like our family that resided in the city of Chicago. My father was constantly focused on relocating to the area that benefited our family economically.

In the spring of 1954, after the school year ended, we moved to the state of Michigan to work as farm workers. We traveled with another family that was in similar circumstances, but had a car. The two families moved from town to town where crops were in season and where farmers had dire necessity for farm workers to pick their crops. We worked in places like Saginaw and Perry, as well as other small agricultural towns in the area.

At the age of nine years, I was working and getting paid as an adult farm worker. In the early 1950's, it was common to see children working as adults since there were no child labor laws in existence or enforced. This was my family's introduction to the journey known as *las piscas,* the process known as picking crops.

I recall one of the places where we worked. It was a company town which today can be characterized as a Nazi type concentration camp, with totally inadequate housing facilities. Upon arriving, the farm worker families were given housing in exchange for working for this large pickle industry company. The farm workers were told they would be paid in cash for picking cucumbers by the pound. At the end of the working day, the farm workers were led into an area where the farmworker children lined up with their family's sacks full of cucumbers, waiting for company staff to sort, select, and weigh the cucumbers and eventually get paid in cash for the daily product of their family's hard work. Workers were paid only for the cucumbers that were found to be acceptable in terms of size and condition.

Sometimes this process took up to two hours. This was why it was the children that stood in the lines, not the adults. I vividly recall standing in line after having picked cucumbers all day, spending hours waiting to be paid cash for our family's work. The employers, known to us as *los patrones* (the bosses), sometimes told us that more than half of our pickings were "worthless". We knew better, for we would see these so-called worthless cucumbers being taken in produce trucks to be sold in the market.

This process could be characterized as debt peonage, a form of involuntary servitude. In other words, a form of slavery. The company in essence was saying, "welcome, we are here to help you and are very happy to give you work, but in the meantime, please understand that you must pay for housing and food, and by the way, we will not pay you for all the work that you do." My family had become *trabajadores del campo* (migrant farm workers), fieldworkers, a euphemism for slaves working under oppressive circumstances.

I saw how hard my parents were working and how difficult it was for them to keep up with their other obligations with us, especially for my mother, who woke up early in the morning to dress and feed us, and then join us to pick the crops. When she returned from working all day, our mother made sure that we were bathed, she washed our clothing, and she prepared our meals.

All farm worker families went through a similar experience. All work, little rest. It was then that I began to recognize my spiritual connection with the farm working community. To this day, I consider myself to be a farm worker in spirit. The fact that later in life I became an attorney seeking criminal and social justice for the working poor is no coincidence. I never forgot. How could anyone forget?

After the cucumber picking experience, we moved on with a *troquero* (a truck driver) to other farming towns throughout the state of Michigan. A *troquero* was typically a bilingual individual who not only owned and drove a canvas covered semi-large pickup truck, but also served in multiple roles, including acting as leader/spokesman of migrant farm worker families in his care, and as a translator, labor contractor, and broker.

We planted and picked mint, green beans, and other crops, barely affording food and shelter with the meager compensation that my parents received for their hard work.

Throughout these experiences, my father told us that his intent was for our family to eventually go back to Mexico to open up a business. I hardly understood his stated wish to go back to Mexico, since before he had been adamant about leaving Mexico with no intent to return. I truly believe that he was just trying to uplift our spirits so that we could successfully confront this phase of our lives.

Hello, Indiana and Ohio

We left Michigan and moved on to another company town, either in the state of Indiana or Ohio. History would repeat itself

As before, we ended up dealing with a similar debt peonage setting, with no compensation until we had picked all the crops. Even if my father and his co-workers disagreed with the unfair working conditions, they had no choice but to go along with *el troquero*. *El troquero* would continue to make decisions for us.

Not having our own mode of transportation, we were consequently literally stuffed into the back of a truck with four or five other families. The truck was big enough to have a comfortable capacity of about ten individuals, but we would crowd in numbers of twenty or more adults and children during our travels. The conditions inside of the truck, although joyous at times, was sometimes tense when some of the occupant farm workers started to express feelings of desperation and anger, and rightfully so, since the conditions were in no way conducive to necessary privacy, especially at night.

Sometimes, as we travelled at night from town to town in the overcrowded back of the truck, I heard the noises made by certain young couples that felt the need to make love while the rest of us were trying to get some sleep. Surely the couple making love thought this to be a joyful moment for them. For the rest of us, this was just another annoying moment that was disrupting our sleep.

Hello, Arkansas

After months of hard work, my parents accumulated enough money to buy a car, a symbol of well-deserved independence. It was an older problem-ridden car that was hardly drivable. By the end of the summer, my father decided that we would go back to Texas on our own. I was proud of my father having made this decision on his own, without depending on the *troquero* or anyone else for that matter, even though we were still connected to him via the caravan of farm worker families.

On our way to Texas, I remember passing through Little Rock, Arkansas and listening to the incessant sounds of police sirens throughout the night. Unbeknownst to us, there were riots throughout the city at the time due to civil rights protests.

It was between Arkansas and Houston where we had our first experiences with African-American farm workers. We lived in a swamp area that was converted into a cotton field, with houses built on wooden stilts to prevent flood damage. We were so close to the river that we could see what appeared to be crocodiles during our usual games of hide and seek.

The black families coming into the fields looked at us strangely, with suspicion and what must have been a sense of fear of competition. Somehow, some African-Americans told us to move on, to leave the area, while others defended our right to work. We stayed no more than a week or so because we were told the cotton crop was not as productive that year as it had been in the past years. We moved on to Texas with still another *troquero,* but following him in our own car.

Hello, Houston

On our way to Texas, my father became ill, landing him in the hospital overnight. To make matters worse, our car broke down, forcing us to rejoin the *troquero*. As usual, every time we arrived in a new town, we usually relied on the *troquero* to find us shelter and other needs. While the adults attended to the basic needs of the groups (finding work, food, and planning the financial situation), the kids would spend time waiting and playing.

In Houston, much like in other cities, we played games such as *La Loteria*, a Mexican form of bingo. Once again, our family was in a new town with not much more than the clothing on our backs. We had sold our car for next to nothing, and paid the *troquero* to take us to the next town to find a distant relative. I remember my father looking at my mother and raising the question *"Y ahora que?"* ("And now what?").

Luckily, my father located the family friends (my grandmother's *comadre*), and was able to reach them by phone. The person who responded to the phone call was receptive to the idea of picking up our family and taking us back into their home where we stayed until my father found work in Houston as a laborer. The host family members were very kind and hospitable, which of course, made us feel welcomed.

We went to school for about a month or so before my father decided to move back to Eagle Pass, Texas, our starting point a year before. At the time, this decision turned out to be the best for our family. My father had surrendered to the reality that riding this horse, taking his family to las piscas en el norte (picking crops in the north), was not working out and it was time to dismount!

After twelve months of following the so-called road to riches, we had gone full circle with nothing to show for it in terms of financial gain. On the other hand, those twelve months of life experiences were worth gold in terms of lessons learned: *No hay mal que por bien no venga* (Every cloud has a silver lining). I was just happy to be back in Eagle Pass and close to Piedras Negras, the town where I was born and raised.

LESSON LEARNED

- Nothing is permanent except change. The best way to respond to change is to adapt to it.

CHAPTER 5

Remembering the Border Town of Eagle Pass

During the 1950's and earlier, Eagle Pass, Texas (also known then as *El Aguilon* and *El Paso del Aguila*) was truly a Mexican-American town along the Texas/ Mexican border. It was American in the sense that it was socially, economically and politically controlled predominantly by white Anglo-Saxon Americans, whom we referred to as (*Americanos or gringos*). It was Mexican in the sense that the population of Eagle Pass was predominantly of Mexican heritage. The political power players of the city believed in a racial segregation, cowboy type approach of living in the wild west and acted accordingly. It was a stratified society, a microcosm of the state of Texas, personifying the good, the bad, and the ugly mindset that Texas had to offer.

Many residents of Eagle Pass would act their part as *Tejanos* (Texans), or Americans in a way that reflected this mindset on a daily basis. Famous Mexican painter Frida Kahlo used to refer to *gringos* as *gringachos,* but that's another story. Most of the time, the Texans of Mexican decent and *Mejicanos recien llegados* (newly arrived Mexican immigrants) were on the sidelines even though they constituted the majority of the local population.

Typical house we rented in Eagle Pass from October to mid-May.

Upon returning from *el Norte* (the northern states of the United States) to Eagle Pass in late autumn, migrant parents immediately enrolled their kids in school. In Eagle Pass, migrant families integrated into a community that was receptive to the immigrant/migrant worker population coming back from *el Norte,* after the summer months, because of the substantial temporary positive impact that the migrant worker families had on the town's economy. On the other hand, Eagle Pass local government officials felt the burden of having to provide additional infrastructure and other necessary social services to the migrant worker community for the next six months, until it was time again for the migrant worker families to leave Eagle Pass to go north. This annual situation sometimes created tense social, cultural, and political conflict.

During this period in the 50's, the power players in the city always made it clear that it was the white men that controlled Eagle Pass. This is why it was not surprising that, in Eagle Pass schools, in the 50's, we as Mexican students were not allowed to speak Spanish during classroom hours and sometimes even during recess. Those students that dared to violate the no-Spanish policy, intentionally or unintentionally, were subjected to a monetary fine of a penny or nickel per violation and, if the violations continued, the violators were subjected to corporeal punishment practices such as a spanking with a wooden paddle.

Recently I was told by a former student that she was subjected to the paddle more than twenty times when she was in third grade in Eagle Pass. Since Spanish was her native language, it came natural to her to speak Spanish while playing at recess. She further told me that she and other female class-mates would use extra petticoats to soften the impact of the paddle. At the same time that Mexican students were not allowed to speak Spanish, the sons and daughters of white Anglo-Saxon leaders of the community were taken out of the regular classroom in elementary school during school hours to be taught Spanish in another classroom.

I later found out that these Anglo-Saxon children were being trained to be *patrones* (bosses), the future business owners, supervisors and otherwise lead-ers in Eagle Pass. Another example of this obnoxious practice was the selec-tive process that was used to ensure that Anglo-Saxon students were always selected to participate in the best educational events in the school system. These reprehensible practices were carried out even though the vast majority of the student body population was not Anglo-Saxon. Nonetheless, in spite of racist practices by white Anglo-Saxon administrators, many Mexican and Mexican-American students eventually graduated from high school, attended college, and became quite successful later on in life.

Recently my wife and I attended the celebration of our 50th Class Reunion of Eagle Pass High School and confirmed the success stories. What was inter-esting was that our classmates felt as we did in regards to giving more credit to individual teachers rather than to the school district policies/practices and top administrators for the eventual academic or professional success of Eagle Pass alumni.

While attending Eagle Pass elementary schools, newly arrived *Mejicanos* like myself faced plenty of bullying, ostracizing, and marginalizing carried out by students that did not see us as belonging in the Eagle Pass community. During and after school hours, I often got into physical fights simply because I was considered to be an outsider. Suffice to say, my social life in Eagle Pass elementary schools was not a good one. I looked forward to weekends when we would go *al otro lado* (the other side) to visit our relatives in Piedras Negras, the place where I felt more comfortable.

The exception to my bad school experience(s) in Eagle Pass were the two years I spent in Eagle Pass Junior High School. These two years turned out to be the most memorable and gratifying in terms of my educational experience in Eagle Pass. The Junior High school teachers that I was fortunate to have were most dedicated when it came to responding to our educational needs as immigrants. These teachers, who ironically were mostly non-Latinos, were truly culturally competent because they understood us as immigrants, they were sensitive to our educational needs and they respected us as human beings. These teachers had the heart and soul to teach us as normal typical students. Bottomline, these teachers were certainly rare and worthy of admiration.

I remember Mr. Garza, a great reading teacher who doubled up as a school bus driver and Mr. Dickerson, my homeroom teacher, who used humor as an effective teaching tool. I remember Ms. Kennedy, the strictest, but the best math teacher in the world. In Ms. Kennedy's classroom, there was no room for failure. In recognition of her teaching success, the Eagle Pass community eventually named a Junior High School building in her honor. I remember two Latina teachers, Ms. Riddle and Ms. Jiménez, who taught language classes with the goal of ensuring that their students became eloquent in Spanish and in English. I also remember Mrs. Graham, an English teacher who would go beyond the call of duty to ensure that students recognize the value of education. At one point, Mrs. Graham taught us to learn and recite the following poem: "Silver and gold will fade away, but the beauty of learning will never decay". I forgot the author's name, but I will never forget the poem or Mrs. Graham. I also remember Mr. Smith, our science teacher who would invite his students to his home to see and explore the universe through a telescope that he installed in his backyard. I remember Ms. Nelson, our eighth grade English teacher, who would make English an enjoyable subject to learn.

Then there was Coach Hogan, the Eagle Pass High School head football coach who doubled up as a Jr. High School history teacher. Mr. Hogan was most popular because of football, *a la* Texas style. His teaching style reflected his coaching style - he would like you as long as you did what he wanted you to do.

On one occasion, Mr. Hogan was giving a history lecture on the Cuban Revolution and I openly, but with all due respect, or so I thought, contradicted him regarding some factual information about Fidel Castro, the Cuban Revolution leader. As I was expressing my point of view, I sensed that Mr. Hogan was fuming. I felt that I was correct regarding my facts but I failed to recognize the refrain, "Sometimes you may be right, but you are going to be dead right!". When I finished making my point, Mr. Hogan told me to follow him to the hallway outside of the classroom. Mr. Hogan took from the top of his desk a double wooden paddle, a punishment tool used by teachers in the 50's, and proceeded to ask me to bend down. He then used the paddle on me three times and told me that I had a choice of going back to the classroom and sit down and not say anything or I could choose to go home immediately. I responded that I would prefer to go home immediately and so I left. Mr. Hogan became angrier and went back to the classroom. Enough said about academic freedom of thought and academic freedom of expression.

A year later, as a freshman in high school, I expressed interest in playing football to one of the coaches and he took me to Mr. Hogan's office. Mr. Hogan recognized me and said to his assistant coach - "I know this kid. He has a good head on his shoulders and can be mean. He will make a good half-back". Although I did not play much football that year, I felt vindicated. These Jr. High School teachers in Eagle Pass really inspired me to do more towards my goals and as a result, I always felt very fortunate and grateful for these Jr. High school years in Eagle Pass.

Social life in Eagle Pass came alive due mainly to the Mexican cultural festive influence. Once a year on the week of Washington's Birthday in February, Eagle Pass and Piedras Negras city officials, with the cooperation of the American and Mexican governments, joined to celebrate the *Dia de la Amistad Internacional* (International Friendship Day), a full day of joint festivities on both sides of the border.

On that particular day, normally a Saturday, the border passage was toll free and the main festivity was a big parade that included marching bands from both sides of the border. The American bands marched across the international bridge into Mexico to the main plaza, where school bands from several different Mexican towns joined them, and then both American and Mexican bands marched back across the international bridge into Eagle Pass as if the border did not exist. All the downtown merchants on both sides of the border would prepare for this festive day because it meant a big day for business and consumers alike.

Local restaurants like the Eagle Hotel coffee shop, the Charcoal Grill, and the Cactus Cafe attracted residents from Mexico and residents of Eagle Pass would go to the restaurants across the border into Mexico in Piedras Negras. Furthermore, going to the movies was fun in Eagle Pass. You had the choice of going to the Aztec, the Yolanda, and the Iris walk-in theaters or, if you wanted to go to a drive-in movie theater, you could go to the Eagle Drive-In or the El Cenizo Drive-In.

As a kid growing up in Eagle Pass, I was not interested in the political affairs of the city. However, the names of prominent political figures would come up in adult conversations that I overheard. A name that I heard frequently was Judge Bibb, who just happened to be not only the County Judge for the County of Maverick where Eagle Pass is located, but was also the Chair of the County Commission, as well as the Chief Maverick County Administrative Officer. Talk about political power and conflicts of interest. Not necessarily *a la Judge Roy Bean* (an eccentric late 1800's American saloon-keeper Justice in adjacent Val Verde County) who called himself "The Law West of the Pecos", but pretty close to it. But then again this was Texas, otherwise sarcastically referred to as The Republic of Texas.

For us kids, the most prominent person in Eagle Pass was Monico, *el paletero,* (the ice cream man), who always wore a safari style hat and khaki shirt and pants (to protect himself from the sun and heat), and peddled a tricycle style vehicle all around town. Perhaps not as powerful as Judge Bibb, but Monico always brought us joy with the ringing of his bell announcing his arrival and his smiling face plus, of course, the delicious popsicles and ice cream that he sold.

As a 14-year old living in Eagle Pass, I began to consider the city on the other side of the border, Piedras Negras, from a different perspective. I was an adolescent who, being a human being, was developing hormone-wise. One open secret that prevailed in Eagle Pass (at least amongst young men) was that, if you wanted action sex wise, you could get action in Piedras Negras. The culture in Mexico then was male dominated and driven by a belief that women existed in this world only to serve or accommodate men. This belief was evident at all levels of Mexican society and the social culture in Piedras Negras was no exception.

Every Mexican border town had a tolerance for prostitution in every form. The rationalization went along the notion that decent females had to be protected so that at time of marriage, these females would still be virgins. Based on this rationalization, Mexican society was tolerant of male sexual activity in areas referred to as *zonas rojas* (zones of tolerance). In Piedras Negras, the ladies of the night had a designated place where they could sell their services. These places ranged from *la zona roja* to *cantinas* that used *ficheras* (token users) and *casas de cita* (designated houses that rented rooms in residential areas). If you wanted sex and could pay for it, you could get plenty of it. Even prisoners at the local jail were allowed to have conjugal visits for that purpose.

It was almost an open secret that almost every young man would go through a sex training session of sorts. The immediate family of the young man designated, in a discrete manner of course, a family member such as an uncle to do the training. Seldom did a father do the training of his son(s). For young men that lived in Eagle Pass and had relatives in Piedras Negras, this was heaven on earth. Enough said about these particular youthful experiences in Eagle Pass and Piedras Negras. I did not do it and if I did, there is no evidence that I did.

Each autumn that we returned to Eagle Pass from other states, my parents rented a house near the downtown area and close to the international river. The river was known to Americans as the Río Grande and to Mexicans as the Río Bravo. The river was appropriately named Grande for its size and Bravo because of its rough waters. In the 1950's it was customary for those who did not have immigration documents to swim across the river, an act that ultimately led to the creation of the pejorative term wetback. The people that crossed the river used a pathway by our house that stemmed from the river to the main road. The main road led to the railroad station where the immigrants caught the early train out of Eagle Pass to inland American destinations.

My father, having been in this country as an undocumented worker himself, was very compassionate when assisting others similarly situated individuals. I vividly remember one occasion, at about two in the morning, when everybody in our house was awakened by a frantic knock on our door. When I opened the door, there stood a fully naked man asking for help, for he had lost his clothes while crossing the river. It was common for those trying to cross the river to carry their clothes over their head while swimming across the river. Sometimes, the rough waters would cause them to lose their clothing while in the process of trying to swim across the river. Since it was very cold outside, my father immediately asked my mother to get a blanket for our naked guest. My mother started to make coffee as well. The man was in our house for about an hour while we clothed and fed him. Soon thereafter, my father drove the now fully clothed man to the railroad station, just in time to catch the early morning train out of Eagle Pass. This type of occurrence was not unusual during this time. The knocks on the door would reoccur quite a few times during our stay in this particular house close to the river. My parents always assisted the people who showed up on our doorstep with the utmost respect and understanding.

Our rented house by the river path where we were waken-up by a frantic knock on the door.

This is how I remember the Eagle Pass of the 1950's.

LESSON LEARNED

- Your youth is the foundation of your character; youth moments are always teachable moments to be enjoyed for they disappear so swiftly.

CHAPTER 6

Hello, California

At the end of every school year in Eagle Pass, from 1955 to 1961, my family migrated to the Santa Clara Valley in California to work in the fields and in the canneries. Once again, my father was convinced that California was where the gold could be found. In late May of 1955 we moved to the Santa Clara Valley, the Valley of The Heart's Delight, now known as The Silicon Valley. Some farm worker families in the Eagle Pass community had indicated to my father that working in the fields, picking fruit around the San Jose area in California, rewarded workers with more than adequate compensation. My father now believed that going to California was smarter than traveling to *el norte*, to places like Michigan and other northern states. Given the disastrous work experiences in Michigan, Indiana and the other states, my father was correct in drawing this conclusion.

As we travelled with another family to San Jose, California in the spring of 1955, we were subjected to a series of quite unfriendly USA Border Patrol roadblocks. Thousands of undocumented and documented Mexican workers were deported as a result of these roadblocks. These actions, on the part of the Border Patrol, were clearly a reflection of the political anti-immigrant sentiment that was expressed throughout the USA during the mid 1950's and especially throughout the Southwest states. Welcome to the United States of America!

These and other anti-immigrant actions were typical in an era of mass deportation of undocumented workers. The Border Patrol persecuted us to enforce the law regardless of our actual legal status in the United States. These reprehensible type of enforcement methods were clearly unconstitutional and contrary to the principles of freedom, liberty, and the pursuit of happiness.

The presence of the Border Patrol instilled in our family a tremendous amount of frustration, humiliation, fear, and plain terror despite the fact that we had been legal residents for some time.

On one occasion when my family was traveling to San Jose with another family, we stopped to eat at a restaurant in Marfa, Texas, southeast of El Paso, Texas. As we approached the entrance to the restaurant, we noticed two signs on the window by the door that read, **"We reserve the right to refuse service to anyone",** along with another sign just beneath that plainly stated, **"NO DOGS OR MEXICANS ALLOWED".**

It was not surprising to me to see the signs. I had seen similar signs before. What was surprising to me was that no adults in our families made any effort whatsoever to challenge the sign or the restaurant's policies or practices towards people of Mexican descent. The adult members of our families basically read the signs, turned around, and left without hesitation.

I began to recognize then that racism was not only prevalent in these parts of Texas, but that the victims (our own family members) were surprisingly passive in their reaction to these clearly overt practices of racial discrimination. For whatever reason, our family members had become accustomed to, or had been conditioned to being victimized, accepting the situation as a reality not to be dealt with other than by walking away from it. What a waker-upper! I felt hurt and humiliated by this experience, even at a tender age of ten.

As we approached El Paso and Ciudad Juárez, two large border cities, one, El Paso, Texas, and the other one, Ciudad Juárez, México, I began to wonder how people in these two cities dealt with the different cultures of each other. My parents decided to take us across the border into Mexico to eat at a Mexican restaurant in Ciudad Juárez. As it turned out, this was a very enjoyable experience, seeing that we were back in Mexico for a brief time, eating without concern of our skin color or ethnicity. Not knowing whether we would return in the future, we fully, and I mean fully, enjoyed *flautas* and *tortas* with cream and *guacamole*.

We proceeded on to San Jose through the desert cities of Phoenix, Tucson, and Yuma. When we arrived in San Jose, we were pleasantly surprised to see the difference of green pastures and orchards as opposed to the desert-like, sparse terrain of Texas, New Mexico, and Arizona.

When we arrived in California, we were dropped off at a ranch just south of San Jose, in the tiny town of Coyote, California and found ourselves in a situation where we had to ask the owner of the ranch if we could stay and work in the fields picking strawberries. The owner of the strawberry farm was gracious enough to receive us, indicating that we could stay in a separate abandoned and dilapidated house, with no windows, electricity, or running water not far away from his own home. My parents assigned me the responsibility of gathering firewood around the house and nearby area to start a fire for heating and cooking.

Strawberries were easy enough to pick, but very strenuous on our backs, especially on the backs and knees of my parents. Without doubt, the job of picking strawberries proved easy enough for child workers, but much more difficult for adults.

Once our family made enough money within the first week to buy groceries, we got a ride to go to a San Jose grocery store that many Mexican families frequented because the store sold condiments that were traditional for Mexican foods. Fortunately, and by pure coincidence, my father ran into a cousin of his named Amaro Villarreal. It had been years since they had seen each other. El Tío Amaro had been living in San Jose with his family for several years. He was not only happy to see us, but was ready and willing to assist us in any way possible. After telling us that there was a better place to work and live than our current location, Tío Amaro took us to see a farm labor contractor by the name of Martín Moralez to see if we could, as a family, be hired as farm workers.

Tío Amaro and Tía Maria Villarreal with family, December 1955.

Don Martín, as he was referred to out of respect, was known for always dealing with people in a helpful way. Despite the fact that Don Martín did not know how to read or write, he had become a successful farm labor contractor by hiring hundreds of farm workers to pick fruit crops in the Santa Clara Valley. He had developed a very effective support system that included his wife, Ruth, known to her friends as Doña Cuquita. She attended to the needs of his single migrant workers (employees and renters) by preparing daily meals and doing their laundry. Don Martín talked to us and readily offered our family work and housed us in a small house behind his own home. We stayed in Don Martín's compound for the summer, picking cherries and apricots until my parents found work in the local canneries, company factories where fresh fruits and vegetables were canned.

Later, I found out that, during the mid 50's, there were approximately thirty-six canneries in the Santa Clara Valley, each one with three working shifts (24-hour period), employing thousands of people in the Valley, making it fairly easy for my parents to find work around the area. At that time, there were few child labor laws, and, if laws existed, few if any, were enforced. Therefore I, just as other children my age, worked just as hard as an adult, picking crops in the summer sun. Despite the hard work, I fully enjoyed that summer of 1955 in California.

At the end of October, we returned to Eagle Pass and, once again, my mother enrolled us in school. Although we had missed a couple of months of schooling, just as many other children that had followed the crops with their parents to *el norte* had done, my sisters and I were happy to be back in school.

In the springtime of the following year, as soon as school was out, we returned to San Jose to work in the fields and in the canneries, just as we had done the year before. This would be the routine for our migrant family for the next six years. While in Eagle Pass in the winter months, my parents barely survived financially by doing odd jobs and taking care of us as we attended school.

The Teachings of Don Martín

In the summer of 1957, when I was twelve, we went back to San Jose to work and live with Don Martín and his family. One day, as I was working and playing with other kids in the orchards while our parents were working, Don Martín approached me and indicated to me that he would teach me how to work. He said to me, "Don't play with the other kids anymore, you are going to learn how to work. I am going to teach you how to work". As it turned out, I was not the only one that he had trained to work. Don Martín, unlike other farm labor contractors, enjoyed teaching others how to work. Although illiterate and with a lot of other job responsibilities, Don Martín was willing to give up his time to teaching others how to do specific work and how to work with the other workers. Without doubt, Don Martín knew his stuff about working with fruit trees.

Don Martín Moralez and his wife Ruth (Doña Cuquita) in the 1950's

The first thing Don Martín did was to direct me to an apricot tree and asked, "Do you see this tree? This tree may be just another fruit tree on first sight, but you have to understand that this tree is here to produce fruit every year. This fact makes this tree a very special and valuable tree. In order for this tree to produce more and better fruit every year, you as the fruit picker must learn to be sensitive to the needs of the tree and respect the tree. I'm going to show you how to pick fruit from this tree". Don Martín continued to show me how to treat the tree correctly, teaching me how to avoid touching and damaging the tree with the ladders we used to pick the fruit off the tree. I realized then that he was very serious about teaching me how to work correctly and he did just that. I learned how to work hard and put in the effort towards learning how to work correctly.

*As a young man I was picking grapes in Pleasanton, California with
Don Martín, in the summer of 1958*

Two years later, when I was 14 years old, Don Martín said to me, "Now that you know how to work, I am going to teach you how to manage people". He began to teach me how to approach, to communicate effectively and to connect with individuals and groups alike. He wanted to make sure that I became a competent, efficient supervisor of workers. To put me to the test at 14 years of age, he assigned forty (40) farm workers to work under my supervision. I began to supervise adults that had come from multiple backgrounds and different regions of Mexico. Don Martín turned out to be a great mentor.

Later, in my professional life as an attorney administrator, when I was asked where I had acquired the knowledge and skill necessary to supervise attorneys, I didn't cite a college classroom training session or university degrees. I cited Don Martín, the man who taught me how to manage people working in the orchards of the Santa Clara Valley in California. Don Martín said that he had learned what he knew in *The University of Life*. He knew how to count, he knew how to negotiate, he knew how to plan, he knew how to execute, but most importantly, he knew how to connect with people. In essence, he knew all of the management and leadership methods and practices that university professors teach today. Don Martín acquired these management and leadership skills by working everyday with hundreds of people, skillfully getting people do what he wanted them to do, and always doing it in a very respectful way. Don Martín was truly a self-educated man and a great mentor to me and many other individuals.

On a daily basis, I and the crew of workers I supervised, traveled to different orchards and worked with the orchard owners as agreed upon by Don Martín and the orchard owners. One day, we arrived at a particular apricot orchard in Cupertino, California. Upon arrival, I approached the owner and told him that we were ready to begin picking the fruit. The owner indicated to me that he would not be paying us the amount of twenty-two cents a bucket that we had expected, but that he was ready to pay twenty cents per bucket of picked apricots. Originally, he had agreed with our labor contractor, Don Martín, that we would be paid twenty-two cents per bucket. Later, he had simply changed his mind or never intended to pay what he had promised.

I returned to the workers and, with everyone gathered around me, told them in Spanish that the *patron* (the boss) would not be paying us what we had expected. The orchard owner had told us to take it or leave it. As I looked around to sense a reaction by the workers, I noticed that many workers were silent, some displaying a look of frustration and even anger.

During this time of economical need, two cents per bucket was a huge difference in compensation for their work. Most farm workers were being paid a dollar per hour because it took about an hour to pick five buckets. We all knew this. The workers asked me, a fourteen-year-old kid, whether or not I thought that twenty cents per bucket was a reasonable wage for their work. As I looked back at them, I felt that they were seeking direction from me in this very crucial moment. I pondered the question for a few seconds and responded, "No, I think that we deserve twenty-two cents a bucket and we should refuse to take the offer of twenty cents a bucket". The workers then asked me, "Now what?". I told them that I would return to the owner and tell him that we were going home, since twenty cents a bucket was not what he had promised us. I returned to the farmer and told him what we had decided to do. With a straight face, he said, "Okay, that's your decision". As I turned to leave, I walked only a few steps before hearing, "Hey kid!". As I turned around he said, "We'll pay you twenty-two cents a bucket". When I returned to the workers and relayed the new offer, actually the original offer, the workers shouted, "*Vamos a trabajar!*" ("Let's get to work!"), with happiness displayed on their faces.

Fighting for the right to work for a decent wage meant fighting for the right to live, to eat, and to care for our families. The day was a victorious day for us. Although this glorious moment was brief, it proved to be a milestone in the pursuit of my professional future as an advocate for social justice. This was truly a leadership moment for me.

LESSONS LEARNED

- Sometimes it is worth putting in your two cents of moral leadership courage, even if it is for two cents a bucket.

- We certainly are not in a post-racial era; racism is alive and well!

- Respect the elderly for they are pathfinders; they have traveled where we have to travel; they know where it is rough and difficult and where it is level and easy.

- The best manager knows how to select the right workers and knows when to leave them alone to do their job.

CHAPTER 7

Hello, East Los Angeles and East San Jose

Early in 1957, my father abruptly decided that we were to move to Los Angeles, California during our school year. Upon arriving in L.A., my father, always being super resourceful, found an address of a distant relative and reached out for his relative's assistance. Asking distant relatives for help upon entering a new city became a beneficial pattern for my father.

As soon as my parents found work, we moved into our own rented place. My father was very good as a provider and my mother was a very good support system for him.

Our stay in Los Angeles, needless to say, caused a high degree of turmoil in my life. We moved to a little apartment behind a large house on the corner of First and Indiana Streets in East Los Angeles in a neighborhood that was known as Belvedere. Unbeknownst to our family, in 1957 the Belvedere area in East Los Angeles was famous, or rather infamous, as a very dangerous gang populated area in the greater Los Angeles area.

Back in the early 1900's, the community of Belvedere was the entry point for newly arrived Mexican immigrant families coming to the Los Angeles area in search of the American Dream. Belvedere was a typical *barrio* where Mexican families were usually striving to make ends meet. Most families were working hard but were not attaining their basic goals economically. As in other *barrio* communities in other major cities, opportunities were limited for those in poverty and with limited education. In essence, Belvedere was just another *barrio* much like the *barrios* in the other cities where we had previously lived, that is, a community where its residents were not in control of their economic, political, or social destiny.

Most Belvedere residents lived in congested, dilapidated, and rodent infested rental homes owned by slumlords who failed to maintain the homes while charging an exorbitant rental fee for them. I was just content that my father kept on expressing the idea that someday we, as a family, would do well economically enough to go back to Mexico.

The next six months of living in Belvedere proved to my father that his dream of success was becoming almost a nightmare, not only to him, but especially to me. When my mother enrolled me in Belvedere Elementary School, in the middle of my sixth-grade year, I noticed that most kids my age were in one way or another involved in gang related activities such as gang fights, vandalism and petty theft.

On numerous occasions, a classmate whom I assumed was a gang member, approached me with the intent of recruiting me to join a particular gang. Since I was not close friends with this particular classmate, I listened to him with caution. The street smarts that I had learned as a result of living in Mexico and Chicago were paying off.

Within a few weeks, I began to build a friendly relationship with another classmate named Henry whom I began to trust enough to ask questions about gangs in general. Henry, a *pocho* (a bilingual/bicultural Latino, born and raised in California) had quite an extensive knowledge about gangs in Belvedere although he was not a gang member himself. What was surprising to me was how Henry was able to get along with classmates that were gang members from different gangs. I thought that perhaps Henry's family was a gang family. I did not know nor was I about to ask. All I knew was that Henry was well respected by members of different gang members and that, as long as I was with Henry during school hours, I would not be bothered by anyone in any negative way.

Henry was always very cautious in his responses to my questions, but was specific enough to scare the hell out of me when it came to explaining the rules that the gangs had. For example, Henry said that every gang expected total loyalty from its members, even more loyalty that a member had to his own family. Another rule that was expected to be followed was that once you became a member of a gang, you could not leave the gang and if you tried to leave the gang, you or a member of your family would be killed. Up to this point I had not understood the serious nature of what Henry meant, but based on what I had seen and heard in the first few weeks of school, I knew what these gang members were capable of doing.

At the end of our conversation regarding gangs, I simply asked Henry, "What do I do if I am asked to join a gang?". Henry responded that I should take as much time as I could get to give an answer and that he would carry the message back to the gang(s) that I was thinking about joining. At this time, it actually occurred to me that Henry might be a recruiter for the gangs. I went into panic mode.

My first dilemma was whether to tell my parents. At that time, my parents were both working all day during the school day. I had to find a way to deal with the situation, either by choosing a gang to join, and there were several gangs to choose from, or not joining any of them and facing the possible serious consequences of my decision. This was truly a fight or flight situation. I had never been as frightened as I was during this period of time in my life. I had been surprised by how well these gang kids were able to hide their true persona within the classrooms. From an outside view, these kids seemed to be more or less normal and well behaved. After school, these same kids engaged in gang activities that I surely did not want to participate in.

After much contemplation, I concluded that joining a gang was not a good option, especially given what I had heard about the ominous gang rules. I decided to take the flight option. I also decided not to say anything about my situation to my parents.

Part of my plan was to find a place where I could be safe at least from the hours of 3:00 to 6:00 p.m. After 6:00 pm, my parents would be home from work. I had noticed a public library during my walks around school, and considered the possibility that it was gang-free territory, given the fact that I had not seen any of the gang members going to the public library after school. I decided that the best plan was to run to the public library as fast as I could after school hours, then run home as soon as my parents returned from work.

For the next few months, the library became my safe haven, a place to escape the gangs. Eventually, I began to benefit from running and hiding. I would do my homework in the library and I never encountered any gang members in the library. Having to do homework at the public library turned out to be the silver lining of this otherwise bad situation. As my mother used to say, "*No hay mal que por bien no venga*" (every cloud has a silver lining).

At the end of the school year, my father decided that it was time for us to move on to San Jose, and so we did. My friend Henry had bought enough time for me not to join any gangs and my parents never found out about my nightmare. What a relief.

On to San Jose, Again

The following four years consisted of traveling between Eagle Pass, Texas and San Jose, California. I was doing better in school. I missed Mexico, and I worried that learning the English language would somehow distance myself from my original heritage and culture. But, as my parents would suggest, it was most beneficial for me to embrace the American culture in order to be successful in the United States of America.

During the summer of 1961, before beginning my junior year in a San Jose high school, I approached my parents expressing my wish to stop the migrating routine of moving back and forth between Texas and California. My experiences in the Eagle Pass High School were not generally positive and I felt that I would have better opportunities by staying in San Jose, because the San Jose area had colleges and universities. My parents rejected the idea of my staying in San Jose immediately. They felt that working in San Jose in the summer and returning to Eagle Pass for the winter months was working out for our family just fine. I told my parents that if they left, I would stay on my own. They asked with whom, and I responded that I would ask assistance from my Tío Amaro, our relative who had originally helped us when we first arrived in San Jose. Their decision to go back to Eagle Pass appeared to be definite until a week later when they told me that they had changed their minds. My parents indicated to me that the family would stay in San Jose for the winter so that I could finish high school in San Jose. This was definitely a happy day for me.

Just like the schools in San Antonio, Eagle Pass, Chicago, and Los Angeles, the high school I attended in East San Jose was located in a low-income *barrio* neighborhood. The schools that I had attended in other cities were filled with low-income students that came from impoverished families. It seemed to me that the ineffective teachers, by design, were assigned by the school district administrators to these low-income schools. The schools had administrations that ran the schools with indifference towards students, practicing racism, and marginalizing people of color. Schools in San Jose would be different, or so I thought.

On one occasion, I was involved in a stupid fight over a basketball with a white kid my age. As a result, we were both taken to the principal's office, where the vice principal and the principal sat me down to tell me how I was going to be castigated. I was suspended for two weeks, while the other student, whom I felt was primarily at fault, was not subjected to any type of discipline. The vice principal warned me to refrain from, "bringing any gang members to retaliate". This warning took me by surprise. First of all, I didn't have any gang members for friends. Secondly, the accusatory tone made me feel as if I had committed a serious crime that went beyond the violation of a school policy. Then, I begin to think that the fact that the kid that I had engaged in the fight with was white may have been a factor in the school administrator's decision. Justice in America! Of course, I was angry, but as I often did, I suppressed my anger.

On another occasion, during a counseling session with my high school counselor, he suggested that due to my lack of English proficiency, I would do better if I did not go to college and that I should plan to enter the labor work force as soon as I graduated from high school. It was quite apparent to me that this counselor believed that I was just someone who had no academic future beyond high school. Ironically, I had taken and done well in many courses, such as physics and chemistry, subjects that the school offered, which were advanced in terms of academic rigor.

I recall a conversation with my father in which I had asked about his survival as an immigrant who didn't speak the language. His response to me was that he would use smiles and nods, which combined with his light-complexion, provided a non-threatening personality and this allowed him to blend in with those who discriminated against Latinos. I told him that I had chosen a more defiant approach, using my "yes I can" attitude. My parents always labeled me "*terco*" (stubborn). My stubbornness at this point in my life was fueled by my aspirations of graduating from high school and enrolling in college.

During the summer of 1963, upon graduating from high school, I went to work at the California Packing Corporation, also known as the Del Monte Cannery. I was hired as a box repairman. My co-worker had been working at the company for ten years. There were times when the box machines were working just right and we had downtime, during which the workers had a choice to do something else or do nothing. During these downtimes, I found work to do. While my co-worker was resting, I got the broom and swept the floor, cleaned the machines, and did other tasks that weren't required of me. My co-worker became frustrated with my work ethic. He demanded that I stop making him look bad.

After just two weeks of working on this particular assignment, I was informed by one of the managers that I had been selected to become a grease monkey, that is, someone who's assignment was to grease all of the fruit cutting machines in one particular section of the cannery plant. Two weeks after that, I received yet another promotion. My co-worker was bewildered because he was not promoted. As I had learned early in my life, there is always someone looking. My work ethic had been rewarded with due acknowledgement and increased job opportunities for me. I felt great.

During that same summer in 1963, one day as I was walking along a street in downtown San Jose with my sister and her husband, I recognized a girl on the other side of the street. That girl, Enriqueta Garza, and I had gone to the same high school in Eagle Pass a couple of years back. She was walking with her brother and had noticed me as well, smiling at me from afar. Enriqueta and her brother made their way over to us and we began talking.

Enriqueta Garza, summer 1963

Her brother knew my sister from school in Eagle Pass. Enriqueta and I had known each other since the sixth grade, and at times had been in the same classrooms. She told me that she had just graduated in Eagle Pass and was now living and working in San Jose. I told her that I was graduating from high school in a week and that I would be attending San Jose State College the following semester. After this very brief reconnection, I didn't see Enriqueta again until a month later at the county fair. It was here, in San Jose, California, that I began to court my future wife, the beautiful Enriqueta Garza from Eagle Pass, Texas.

LESSONS LEARNED

- Every cloud has a silver lining, so be on the lookout.

- After every storm, the sun will shine.

- Just when you think nobody is looking, there is always somebody looking.

CHAPTER 8

The Turbulent 60's: Unrest, Conflict, Protest

As the fall of 1963 approached, I felt enthusiastic about the future. I had graduated from James Lick High School and was enrolled at San Jose State College, a 15,000-student population college located in the middle of the *barrio* in San Jose, California. Although the Mexican community surrounded the college campus, it was not well represented in terms of the college's student enrollment. San Jose State could have been more receptive to recruiting *barrio* students simply because the students lived so close to the college. However, the administrators of the college, now a university, were apparently more interested in recruiting and enrolling more than a thousand foreign students from Iran, a country that was on good political terms with the USA at that time. For whatever reason, recruiting students from thousands of miles away instead of recruiting students from the local area, just did not seem to make any sense to me. I just felt fortunate to have been allowed to enroll at San Jose State.

During my first semester of college, I registered in the military ROTC (Reserve Officer Training Corps) program, a college based military training program set up to develop commissioned officers for the United States Armed Forces. While in high school, my goal was to serve in the military to serve the country that had adopted me. I had been drawn to the program through conversations I had with classmates who were participating in the program and seemed to like the program's goals. Additionally, the heavy government recruitment efforts by the military service throughout the university at this time made the program seem attractive. I felt that perhaps I would be able to continue college with some sort of financial help. ROTC was seen as a reasonable solution for financial problems that many low-income students were facing; thus, I enrolled in the program. The process of enrollment included a medical check-up. At the end of the check-up, the doctor said to me, "It appears that you have a big heart". I said, "Thank you, I have always been kind to others". He responded, "No, literally, you have an enlarged heart. As other physical exams come up, we will keep an eye on this. In the meantime, you can continue in the program. Good luck". At this time, I was still hopeful that I would be healthy enough to finish the ROTC program and serve my adopted country as a soldier. I was ready to bear arms to defend this country.

As I continued to become more informed about the Vietnam conflict and how the United States was getting more involved in Vietnam, I began to analyze the situation regarding the position that our country was taking and began to wonder whether this war was just, at least from my perspective. Even though I was still a teenager and was somewhat wet behind my ears about these political matters, I started to ask meaningful questions about the USA engagement in Vietnam. I begin to lean towards the anti-war standpoint that was starting to spread throughout the college campus. I finally made the decision to reconsider my involvement in the ROTC program and decided to end my participation in the program.

When I met with the officers in charge of the program to discuss my decision to resign from the program, they tried to sell me on the idea of staying in the program by pointing to various program benefits and incentives offered by their officer program. Without question, I felt that I was being pressured. The country was preparing for an expanded Vietnam war, and the American military draft program had already begun its effort to expand recruitment of prospective military officers. When I indicated to my local ROTC commander that I had decided to leave the program, he immediately gave reference to my strong leadership abilities. Recognizing that I was not biting, he told me that I most likely would be drafted anyway.

Nonetheless, he invited me to sit down with him on a certain day for lunch to further discuss the matter. After an hour of discussion over lunch, he said, "Okay, so now that I've answered all your questions and have told you everything, I'm assuming you're going to stay in the program, right?". To which I replied, "With all due respect sir, I will not be staying in the program". Upon hearing my response, the commander stood up, expressed his disappointment with me, gave me a stern look, and left angrily. After one college semester in the program, I formally resigned from the ROTC program.

My leaving the ROTC Program was the right decision on my part given my anti-war position. At the same time, I was receiving disturbing but unconfirmed reports that the majority of ROTC students graduating from San Jose State College were eventually being sent to Vietnam as First Lieutenants or as Squad Leaders and were killed almost immediately, due to lack of proper field training and many other factors. I was later told that more than half of the graduating ROTC classes had died in combat. That included some of my colleagues. I realized that I could still be drafted to serve and decided that if that were the case, I would not resist. I was never drafted. My respects to all that served, especially to those that lost their lives serving our country.

As I continued my education at San Jose State, I sought a field of study that would appeal to me. I changed my major from Industrial Technology to Spanish and a minor in French, with the new goal of teaching these two languages at the high school level.

In order to make ends meet, I worked as a Spanish tutor and as a salesman selling cutlery for a company named Cutco (Alcoa Aluminum). I, just as other students, was so financially unstable that I felt that I needed several part-time jobs to help my parents to stay afloat financially. During the summers between school semesters, I worked at the canneries and in the fields.

Ironically, I was learning more about how to navigate through life's challenges by working in the fields and selling those Cutco knives than I ever did in a college classroom. The Cutco experience was more valuable than taking a class in salesmanship. I learned how to connect with people and to develop professional relationships. It took me some time to get comfortable knocking on doors and trying to convince families to buy the over-priced cutlery products that I was trying to sell. The first few weeks of trying to sell knives were somewhat unsuccessful. Actually, my efforts were totally unsuccessful.

After about a month on the job, something clicked. The sales began to pick up. Somehow, I found my voice, learning how to communicate effectively and how to connect through effective communication by reading books such as *How to Make Friends and Influence People* written by Dale Carnegie. I followed the suggested steps in connecting with clients and developing a more positive attitude. The entire process was simplified and almost magical! I was well prepared for my performance, I demonstrated my product effectively, and was able to execute the sales successfully. My self-confidence finally reached a level of comfort, after having suffered several serious self-confidence setbacks in San Antonio, Chicago, Los Angeles, and Eagle Pass. I felt that I was finally regaining my self-confidence.

In the meantime, my relationship with my friend, Enriqueta, was getting stronger. After a little over a year of courting and having to deal with resistance to our getting married by our parents, due to our age and the fact that I was still in college, we got married during semester break on February 6, 1965. During my college years, my wife Enriqueta continued to work with the Pacific Bell Telephone Company. To make ends meet, sometimes my wife and I worked as janitors, cleaning restaurants during early morning hours and sometimes picking crops on week-ends at different orchards in the Santa Clara Valley. During the summer, I worked full-time in the cannery and picking fruit in the fields. All this work experience taught my wife and I to appreciate the value of the work ethic that had been taught to us by our parents. My wife also helped by supporting me emotionally, always encouraging and believing in both of us as a family.

In November of 1965, Enriqueta gave birth to Rolando, our first-born. During the first year and a half of our marriage, we moved our living quarters on five separate occasions, sometimes due to economics and other times because some apartment complexes did not allow children. Our daughter, Meliza, was born in May of 1967. As the world around us was shaking politically, we kept on moving, working towards building a better family life. We were young, full of energy, and ready to take on the world.

To state that the 1960's were turbulent is truly an understatement, even by today's standards. The Vietnam War was escalating, great American patriots like President John F. Kennedy, Martin Luther King, Jr., and Senator Robert F. Kennedy had been assassinated in the 1960's, and Lyndon Baines Johnson had become president. Various anti-war movements were in full swing, political protesters were flooding the streets and the airwaves were expressing sentiments of anti-war protest. On a parallel to the larger efforts of civil rights throughout the United States in 1968, tension was building up on the campus grounds during my last months at San Jose State. There were many political issues confronting the Chicano student population at the university (I am now referring to San Jose State as San Jose State University, SJSU).

When I started my studies at SJSU in 1963, there were only about fifty students that could be labeled Mexicans, Mexican-American, Chicanos, or Latinos. Although we lived in the SJSU campus neighborhood, we never felt welcomed on campus. By 1968, the Latino student population on campus had increased sufficiently to draw the attention of the college administration, but not necessarily in a positive way.

Earlier in my college years, I had declared my major to be Industrial Technology, a combination of engineering and management. I had asked my college advisor about this area of interest, and he was extremely dismissive of my goal. In my mind, I was convinced that I needed to prepare myself to be considered for an administrative position in the near professional future. At this point, I felt that the school education that I was getting was not helping me achieve this goal and felt that the university staff was treating me just as my old high school counselor had treated me, that is, with a high degree of dismissiveness.

Not surprisingly, when I discussed this issue with my Latino colleagues, they expressed that they too had been treated the same way. I began to participate in student meetings to discuss options regarding the direction that the Latino students wanted to take in order to change how the university administration was treating us. My Latino classmates were discussing the possibility of protesting the lack of educational opportunities at the university. We felt that the quality of education that we were receiving was deficient in many respects and, as Mexican-Americans, Chicanos and Latinos, we wanted our future generation students to receive a college education of a higher quality than what we were receiving. As our representatives met with the administration of the university, our representatives demanded cultural awareness and sensitivity programs that would address the needs of our Chicano student population. Our reasonable demands were simply dismissed as unjustified student defiance.

Our protest efforts were reflective of national movements against educational institutional prejudice towards minority groups such as African Americans. We were influenced by leaders such as Dr. Martin Luther King who was leading a strong civil rights movement. At the state level, a

Mexican-American farm worker union leader by the name of Cesar Chavez was leading a fierce fight on behalf of farm workers regarding working conditions. This farm worker movement was inspiring our Latino community to fight for our rights throughout the nation. I do recall that my father-in-law and my mother-in-law, who were farm workers in the San Joaquin Valley at that time, were actively supporting the Cesar Chavez led union.

SJSU Walkout of 1968

At the local level, educationally, we, as college students, felt that San Jose State University did not have staff that was culturally competent to understand us, to respect us, and to be sensitive and responsive to our needs. We felt very strongly that the school administration was totally dismissive and indifferent towards our requests, and we simply grew frustrated and tired of it. As the date of the graduation commencement exercises drew closer, our Latino student groups began to plan a peaceful protest in the form of a walkout during the impending graduation commencement exercises. The organizers were Chicano student leaders who had called meetings to discuss the institutional injustices and the corrective action that the organizers were proposing.

As weeks went by, the number of students, mostly prospective graduating Latino seniors, who were to participate in the protest started to dwindle down from the original thirty. When the university administrators found out about our impending plans for a student protest, they requested the presence of hundreds of riot control police, including U.S. Marshals, state police, and local police to protect the anticipated thousands of commencement attendees at the graduation ceremonies. Given the high degree of anxiety on both sides of the issue, the organizing students were very prudent in their planning to ensure that the protest was non-violent and otherwise peaceful.

The planned Chicano student walkout began to stir up controversy and conflict within myself and among members of our family and friends alike. My family members had expressed discontent with my wife and I for deciding to participate actively in the demonstration by joining the SJSU Walkout of 1968 at the traditional graduation ceremonies. Since I was the first one to graduate from college in both families, everyone in both families expected us to follow tradition in every respect. To walk out, as I was proposing to do, was certainly not traditional.

Latino critics of our proposed protest said, *"Somos gente decente"* ("We are decent people") and claimed that our student action would constitute public shame for the family name and for the Latino community that we represented. On the other hand, our supporters claimed that it was worthwhile to risk shame or disgrace if we were to protest against what we considered social injustice. Some family members had basically failed to understand why I would throw this celebration away to stand up to an institution of higher learning.

Even before the proposed protest became a public controversy, my wife and I struggled within ourselves. We both had anticipated this graduation day for so long with such excitement and had made so many personal sacrifices to reach the finish line. I felt that the graduation ceremony was an important fundamental aspect of both our Mexican and American culture. From my cultural perspective, students were not supposed to deviate from this traditional celebratory process. Although these unanticipated conflicts continued to overwhelm all of us on a continuous basis, my wife and I held steadfast on our decision to participate in the walkout. Upon final consideration of all factors, we concluded that this protest was necessary to help future generations of Latinos who aspire to excel through the formal education process. We were unwavering in purpose.

On the bottom front left, I am walking in with my fellow graduates of SJSU Class of 1968 to participate in the graduation ceremonies.

On the day of the commencement event, June 14, 1968, those of us who were graduating and walking out all felt very nervous and fearful about a potentially violent backlash that could occur during our walkout. None of us were certain how the school officials and the riot control police would react to our protest action. However, in the context of the sixties, we were absolutely certain that the police would not hesitate to physically assault us if we showed any signs of aggressive behavior. Despite our fears of potentially being arrested, we felt that the value of participating in this peaceful protest outweighed the potential backlash. This student protest was certainly the right thing to do.

I continued to explain to our parents that I would not lose my degree certificate, that I would be getting it in the mail, but that this protest was a very worthwhile event that needed to happen. Our parents finally appeared to understand and agreed to support us and even encouraged my immediate family and friends, as the other protestors did, to join us in the walkout of our commencement ceremony.

The walkout plan was to be executed as follows: as soon as the President of the University approached the podium to start his commencement speech, we would stand up in unison and walk towards the exit of the stadium in a quiet and respectful way with our heads up. The expectation was that the riot police would strike us with their clubs, attempting to either stop us, or arrest us, or both. I was actually ready to be subjected to physical injury. As it turned out, the plan that we had developed was effectively executed.

SJSU Graduation Class of 1968

When the time to act arrived, I and eleven other Latino graduating students stood up in front of about fifteen thousand attendees and walked out of our own graduation ceremony before we had gotten the chance to be formally recognized in any manner. A number of college professors and undergraduate students, who sympathized with our cause also walked out with us. As I was walking, I vividly remember focusing on the steps that I was taking while looking up into the bleachers to see where my parents and family members were sitting, just in case something happened to me. My wife and our two children, both sets of parents, my grandmother who came from Piedras Negras, Mexico just for the graduation, and other family members who had come from out of town, also stood up in the bleachers and walked out with us, as did a few other family members of the other graduates.

Our protest was met with silent treatment; nobody moved nor spoke in the fifteen thousand capacity filled stadium. Fortunately for us, the four hundred or so riot law enforcement officers were professional in their approach, allowing us to walk out without incident. As we neared the exit, we started to shout in unison, *"Viva La Raza!"* ("Long live the people!"). An uneasy, fearful feeling in my gut overcame me, anticipating a potentially negative reaction to this misunderstood slogan by misguided minds. But still, no one moved to oppose us, and we were soon safely exiting the stadium.

Once outside the stadium, we held our own private peaceful commencement ceremony and festive celebration directly adjacent to the stadium parking lot. We had done what we had set out to do and we had done it peacefully and respectfully. The several hundred supporters that joined us in the walkout were expressing the same sentiment as we celebrated our college graduation with our families, friends, and Luis Valdez (who had previously graduated from San Jose State University) and his Teatro Campesino, singing and dancing. The celebration continued at my parents' home with family and friends. This event had actually turned out to be a glorious event.

The value of this walkout was greater than we had originally anticipated. The state recognized our action by setting forth actual financial funding for the establishment of Equal Opportunity Programs, as well as the hiring, training, and retention of Latino staff members and faculty in the college. The 1968 Walkout I participated in has been recognized as a significant component of the Chicano movement of the late sixties. Participating in the walkout became a great source of pride in our Latino community during our course of education in this country.

Today, there are numerous Latino commencement exercises throughout the nation, some of which my wife and I have attended in the last few years. The walk-out so inspired, directly or indirectly, our family members that many went on to become educators, administrators, lawyers and business owners, all with a college education. Recently our immediate family attended the Fresno State University Latino Commencement (the largest attended Latino commencement in the nation) where our grandson, Rolando Villarreal, Jr., obtained a degree in English Literature. He is co-editor of this book.

The 60's were the most turbulent and yet the most formative years of my life. My wife and I were undoubtedly happy to have made it through these challenging, yet gratifying years.

LESSONS LEARNED

- You measure twice, you cut once.

- You may be right, but you may be dead right!

- Always hope for the best, but always be prepared for the worst.

CHAPTER 9

Law School, Work, Family, and Poverty

The Law School Experience

During the turmoil times of the 1960's at San Jose State University, the Legal Aid Society of Santa Clara County that provided students legal assistance to address the students' legal issues was now joining the University of Santa Clara Law School in inviting Latino students graduating from the university to enroll in law school. Legal Aid attorneys approached me to apply to the University of Santa Clara Law School the summer of graduation, at which time I had just started working on my masters. Part of the arrangement was that I would be able to work part-time at the Legal Aid Society while I attended law school.

After much consideration and discussion with my wife, I decided to enroll in the law school. In prior years, I had briefly thought about becoming a lawyer; but it never occurred to me that I would ever be granted an actual opportunity to chase that dream.

In September of 1968, I began my first year at law school at the Santa Clara University Law School and started to work as a legal aide at the local Legal Aid Society. At that time, as it is today, the university was a bastion of culture in the Silicon Valley. Socially, economically, and politically, the University of Santa Clara and Stanford University were said to control a Santa Clara Valley that had evolved from being an agricultural-based valley, to become a military-defense industry-based valley. Now it was reinventing itself into the high technology industry-based valley presently known as the Silicon Valley. The law school was traditional in every respect, focusing on legal education at its finest. I attended this private school alongside the sons and daughters of the so called wealthy and elite of Santa Clara Valley. There were one-hundred and twenty students enrolled in the first-year law program, and only two of us were Latino.

The law school was receptive to the idea of "trying out" Latino law students under a new concept known as "Affirmative Action". Under this program, law schools were expected to provide an equal educational opportunity to minority students in the study of law. The expectation was that the affirmative action students like myself had sufficient basic knowledge of aspects of the law. Undoubtedly, in my case, that was not the case. It began to appear to me that the law school faculty was actually trying to insert failure into the affirmative action program, at least in the beginning.

Later on, this so-called affirmation action program became a benign neglect program, a program where the good intentions were expressed but never executed. The lesson that I learned was clear. I had recognized that the law, just as politics, was a very effective tool to achieve social justice. I begin to realize that the "rule of law" was being used to rationalize whatever action was to be taken by the political power players and, as always, those that control the rules of the process control the outcome. For me, the forthcoming experience in law school was like traveling into a brave new world because I was starting off with not only language and cultural barriers but I was coming into such an unknown and unwelcoming environment.

My first year in law school at the University of Santa Clara was undoubtedly challenging, to say the least. Although the law school administration was receptive to an experiment of opening the door to more Mexican-American, Latino, and Chicano students through affirmative action efforts, it was somewhat apparent that the faculty was less inclined to participate in the experiment. Subtle whisper comments such as "Do we really have to do this?" were made and heard in the hallways of the law school. Of course, these statements were never made directly to the Latino students participating in the program.

In addition, I was not able to join the student study groups due to my work schedule. My reality at that time was that I had to balance work, family obligations, and studying on my own. The welcoming committee at the law school, if there was one, disappeared almost immediately. Knowing that the attrition rate for married students was very high, I was making every effort to keep my family together. I was sinking fast trying to keep up with the academic assignments. I was advised to hire a tutor to help me out, but due to my economic limited resources, hiring a tutor was out of the question.

In essence, my first year in law school became an uphill battle that I was to lose. I blamed myself for not being prepared. As a result, I flunked the first year and was told to reapply the following year. The dean of the law school personally indicated to me that he regretted that the faculty and staff were not as supportive as they could have been, although he felt that I had the potential to successfully graduate from law school. This was actually the first time that I had received encouraging words from anyone in the one-year experiment, so I decided to reapply and give it another shot.

That summer, after flunking out of my first year of law school, I was hired by the Redevelopment Agency of the City of San Jose. The Redevelopment Agency was hiring staff to implement a massive urban renewal project in the downtown area. The Redevelopment Agency had been created as a mechanism to enhance the city tax base by developing building projects in areas that were designated as blighted areas. These blighted areas were often barrios where Latinos lived.

In essence, the unintended, or perhaps intended, consequence of these renewal projects was the disappearance of the Latino *barrio* communities. In other words, the powers that be were destroying *barrios* with the idea of renewing the downtown San Jose area. In response to the concerns that were expressed by social community organizations, the Redevelopment Agency assisted the impacted communities in the form of special projects such as affordable housing and affirmative action programs for minority construction contractors and for construction workers in all phases of the renewal projects.

My job as a Contract Compliance Officer was to assist in the development and implementation of affirmative action programs to assist minority contractor/workers. What I acquired from this first real job experience (after graduating from college) was a colossal insight about how American institutions function on a daily basis.

I began to understand how the public sector (the government), the private sector (business), and the social sector (community organizations) engage independently or interdependently to promote and protect their respective interests and, most importantly, I learned how administration, law, and politics come into play in every phase of public project planning and implementation.

The most fascinating thing that I learned is that whoever controls the process, controls the outcome. No wonder the interests of our Latino community always ended last in the priority list. The Latino community simply did not have the economic and political power to control any portion of the process.

As a Contract Compliance Officer, I dealt with city officials such as the city mayor, the city attorney, and other city officials. Since the Redevelopment Agency's projects involved major construction contracts, I dealt with developers, general contractors, union representatives, and community activists. I even had to deal with those that were not interested in serving the public as much as they wanted to serve themselves by engaging in corrupt activities.

One day, I was having a meeting with a construction contractor representative who was aggressively seeking my support in his quest of a huge contract for his employer who was bidding on a multi-million construction contract. At the end of the meeting, I indicated to him that I would get back to him. As he was leaving my office, he placed a white envelope filled with what appeared to be money bills. I asked him what the meaning of the envelope was and he responded that the envelope contained a token of appreciation for me on behalf of his company. I promptly picked up the envelope and placed it in his hand, indicating to him with noticeable anger, that I was not that type of person and for him to take his envelope and leave immediately before I reported him to the proper authorities. He took the envelope and left, never to be seen again. On that day I learned that my parents had taught me well about adhering to ethical principles on the job. Having integrity on the job has always paid off!

Upon returning to law school for a second try in September of 1969, I recognized that I now possessed the necessary skills to continue my law school education. I started taking one or two classes during night school, while continuing to work a 40 plus hour weekly job during the daytime. My wife and I also added to our family two more sons, Adrian (1972) and Alejandro (1973). I eventually accumulated enough credits to graduate in 1974. Pure tenacity, hard work, and the spiritual support of my wife, Enriqueta, were the main reasons why I managed to graduate from law school.

Perhaps it was unreasonable for me to expect some type of assistance from the law school. Perhaps I was angry at myself for not being able to respond to what was expected of me as a law student. Perhaps I was angry at life for not being fair. For whatever reason, I was definitely going through a crisis of low self-confidence.

I had to take the California Bar exam many times before passing it. This nightmare experience turned out to be one of the best teaching moments of my life. I was humbled to a point of no return, but I was able to recover by recognizing that for every problem there is a spiritual solution and, if you are determined and persist accordingly, you will eventually succeed.

The Challenge of Entrepreneurship and Unemployment

By 1976, I had graduated from law school, but had not passed the California State Bar exam. My wife and I decided to sell our house and move from the city of San Jose to the smaller city of Sanger, California. Over the years, my wife and I had visited her parents and other family members in Sanger, where we had been married in 1965, and had decided that it would be better to be close to her family while we got settled into our family life. We wanted to raise our four kids in a small community.

My wife and I managed to go through the challenging process of raising kids with limited financial resources. Unfortunately, when we arrived in Sanger, I was still unemployed. We decided to open a restaurant, much like my parents had done in their professional past. While I was continuing to prepare to take the BAR exam again, we opened a café restaurant named La Villa Real in 1976. On one hand, I was very excited to begin a new venture; on the other hand, I was worried and so afraid of failure. My self-confidence was at the lowest point in my professional life. I had not reached a point of depression, but I was close to it.

After a year of being a restaurant owner and manager, my wife and I decided to look for other employment opportunities because the restaurant was not providing sufficient financial stability for our family. The biggest lesson that I learned as a result of the restaurant experience was that while our business provided food to customers, it was not enough to provide food for our children. It was the first time in my life that I had experienced real financial disaster.

In essence, we had lost all of our life's savings, we were both unemployed, and we had to start all over again financially. This debacle actually forced us to apply for financial aid in the form of welfare, medical assistance and food stamps, for a couple of months. We owed it to our children to put our pride aside and make sure they had medical care and food on the table, because no one would hire me because I was over-qualified. I possessed a law degree, and many employers figured I would leave their organization as soon as I passed the BAR; however, I was not able to practice law because I had not passed the BAR exam at this point. I was stuck. I was too good to work in entry level jobs, and not good enough to work in the field that related to my law degree. I even tried working in the farm labor fields, but it was during the winter and not much work was available for a family of six to survive on.

Since my college graduation in 1968, my wife had been staying home with the children and going to school part-time. Now, the situation called for drastic measures and she went back to work for the telephone company, so that we could get medical insurance for our children. To get off welfare, as I continued to look for employment. We still maintained an active loving relationship with our four children and kept their well-being as a priority at all times.

Lesson learned: Life is not fair. The best option is to keep your head up, to keep the faith, and *Adelante!* (Forward!). Finally, I was able to secure employment with a job development non-profit organization where I was hired as an assistant in the personnel department. Soon thereafter, I was promoted to the position of Personnel Director and I held that job until I passed the Bar Exam. If these experiences were part of a bigger test, my wife and I were certainly ready to take on the rest of the test for we had reached the bottom, financially and psychologically. We had nowhere to go but up.

LESSONS LEARNED

- It is not the situation, it is how you respond to it.

- Those that control the process, control the outcome.

CHAPTER 10

Finding Your Voice

As parents of children attending local schools, my wife and I became increasingly attentive to our daily role in ensuring that our children were attending schools that were adequately responsive to student educational needs. As a result, we became active parents in the Sanger Unified school system by volunteering in classrooms, making observations, and asking relevant questions of teachers and principals about the education of our children.

Through this process, we became aware of an incident at one of our children's school that sparked outrage amongst the Sanger residents. At Lincoln Elementary School, a hyperactive kindergarten student was having behavior issues. He was referred to the school district's psychologist who recommended a practice known as behavior modification which, in this case, basically involved the confinement of a child inside of a cage-like setting within the classroom. The student was literally caged inside of a wooden structure, separating him from the rest of the class and instilling what must have been a deep sense of embarrassment, humiliation, and trauma for the child.

Having kids of similar age as the kindergarten student, my wife and I felt that this school policy and/or practice was horrifying and wondered why it was approved and implemented by the Sanger School District. The kindergarten student had been in our son's class the previous year in a preschool program and as a parent volunteer in that classroom, my wife had been in contact with him on a regular basis in the classroom and a field trip. She felt that he was no different than our kids or other kids. Active yes, but not out of control.

My wife and I decided to join a group of parents who felt the same way we did about the situation. After ample and thoughtful discussion, the group of concerned parents decided to make every effort to stop the school district from continuing to apply the so-called behavior modification policy and practice not only to the kindergarten student, but to any other student as well.

The group of concerned parents in the Sanger School District community set up a series of public meetings with the objective of exposing the school district's practice to the Sanger community in an attempt to rally public outcry towards what we considered to be a clear act of social injustice. Our newly formed ad hoc parent committee held community rallies in downtown Sanger, informing those in attendance about the seriousness of the school district behavior modification policy and practice.

At one particular rally, we, as parents, decided to form a formal committee to seek and find needed volunteers, including an attorney, community work-ers, teachers, and more parents to join us in dealing with what we considered to be a very serious problem in our school district. We got the media involved, and as a result, local television stations, The Fresno Bee, and The San Francisco Chronicle sent representatives to cover the story. The headlines read some-thing along these lines: "Caged Student in Elementary Classroom."

The Sanger school district responded to the situation by being dismissive of our concerns, declaring that the methods applied by the school district to this particular situation were professionally acceptable and effective in chang-ing the behavior of students. The school district took a defensive stance against all media attention, claiming that this was just a misunderstanding. Our parent committee reacted by stating that we would make every effort possible to have the behavior modification policy and practice stop, thus freeing the child of his confinement during classroom hours. Seeking desperate measures in dealing with the school district, we doubled down and threatened a boycott against the school district by keeping students from attending school until the behavior modification practice stopped. The school district continued to be dismissive, continuing to label our reaction as unnecessary.

Moreover, the school principal filed a million-dollar lawsuit against the parent committee, alleging that we were disparaging the school principal's name as a professional educator. Having to confront this lawsuit was very stressful for all of us as parents, since we all were struggling financially and could not imagine how we could afford to pay for a legal defense. Nonetheless, we believed that we were right in our action and we continued to plan the boycott with other parents and members of the community.

Within two weeks, we carried out our action of protest through a two-day boycott. As a result of a well-organized informational campaign, we managed to convince the parents of several hundred students to boycott the school district by not sending their children to school for a few days. The two-day boycott included a protest march of parents and students that was conducted peacefully, but resolute in purpose.

We presented a formal petition at the next school district board meeting demanding that the school district do away with the policy and the practice of behavior modification. Upon recognizing our resolve, the school district finally agreed to cease the behavior modification policy and stopped the practice of placing students in a cage-like confinement. Additionally, the principal of the school agreed to settle her lawsuit against the concerned parents group out of court for twenty-five dollars and a letter of intent on our part stating that we would no longer disparage her image. Our intent was always to stop the behavior modification policy and the practice of the school district. It was about the well-being of our children and never about the principal. The policy and practice of behavior modification was finally stopped. We were victorious.

Looking back at this episode, it becomes imperative to recognize the power of community and civic engagement, the power of peaceful protest, and the power of expression. We, as common folk parents, had taken on a powerful establishment institution, a school district with all its available economic, legal, and political resources. We had protested in a peaceful, effective and successful manner. We had found our voice!

LESSONS LEARNED

- We must recognize the power of civic engagement, the power of peaceful protest, and the power of expression. We must always exercise our right to vote!

- We do not work for public officials, they work for us.

- Fighting injustice for one is fighting injustice for all.

CHAPTER 11

The More You Fail, the Closer You Get to Success

After closing the restaurant business that my wife and I had been involved with for a year, I looked everywhere and finally found an opportunity for employment as a Personnel Director for a non-profit organization in Fresno. Our family managed to escape the welfare experience and I settled down in my job before considering taking the next California State BAR Exam hoping that I would pass it so that I could start practicing law.

Taking the BAR exam is an experience that I do not wish on anyone. To add to its already challenging nature, my wife and I were both working full-time, raising a family of four kids who were very involved in school activities, and I had very little time to study. Was I stubborn in thinking that all I needed was more time? I knew of other law students that had passed the Bar Exam the first time and was frustrated at not knowing why I was not able to pass it other than to suggest to myself that it was just a matter of dedicating more time.

One thing for sure, I learned more about California law during the time that I spent preparing to take the BAR exam than I learned at law school. I had no choice but to try again to pass the BAR exam, which under the circumstances, seemed to be a mission impossible. I concluded that the time had come to decide whether it was worthwhile to continue with the effort. My wife and I had just gone through a failed business venture and we were both wondering whether we could emotionally withstand another failure at this point in our lives.

Taking into consideration all the relevant factors, I decided that this would have to be the last time that I would take the BAR exam. Since this was going to be my last attempt, I decided that I needed to take at least two months to myself, away from work and family, in order to study for the exam and my wife supported me with this idea. We told our children (ages 14, 12, 7, and 6) that things were going to change for a couple of months because I needed to take time off from my job, the family, and my community activities in order to fully dedicate my time to studying. This Bar Exam experience was clearly taking a toll on our family. My dream of becoming a lawyer was still alive, so I was still determined to go through the excruciating process of preparing for the exam.

I continued to ask myself whether what I was doing was selfish on my part. I had struggled to go against the odds and continued taking the test regardless of past failed attempts. Some relatives and friends were suggesting directly and indirectly that I seek a different area of professional interest. Was I riding a dead horse and therefore, it was time to dismount? One thing that I was certain of was that I had my wife's support. She reassured me every time that we discussed the issue that she would support whatever I decided to do. When my wife and I discussed the matter with our children, they responded by saying, "Go for it, Dad." And so, I went for it. No money but plenty of enthusiasm!

We borrowed money from both of our parents, and in May of 1980, I moved to Sacramento, 200 miles away, to live, to study, and to take the Bar exam at McGeorge School of Law two months later. I started taking practice exams and, in the very first exam, I received a failing grade. The very first question that came to my mind was "What the hell am I doing here?" As time passed I got better. I took the exam in July of 1980.

This whole experience had a tremendous negative, emotional impact on me and my family. The silver lining was that I discovered a truism- the more you fail, the closer you get to success! I had read many stories about individuals and companies that had attempted and failed many times before attaining success. I was just hoping that success was within reach.

California State Bar Swearing-In Ceremony, December 1980

Upon returning home from Sacramento, my wife and kids received me with open arms hoping to get back to a normal routine. It was tough on them too, being that we had never been separated like that before. I went back to work and waited anxiously for my test results that were to be mailed to me several months after taking the test. My wife and I were hoping for a thin envelope. A thick envelope (which we were very familiar with) meant that the California State Bar had sent another application form to take the test again, and a letter with the exam results that begin with the words, "We regret to inform you…". When the envelope finally arrived, I gathered my family (wife and kids) around so that we could open it together. The envelope was thin, and we were hopeful. Upon hearing that I had passed the exam, my kids begin shouting, "Yeah! we're so happy for you, Dad!" and other things of that nature. We were all in a group hug celebrating the good news. My wife was crying of happiness and our youngest, Alejandro, asked "Why are you crying, Mom?". She responded by saying "Your Dad passed the BAR exam". His response was, "What does that mean?". My wife said, "It means that your Daddy will never have to study for the BAR Exam again". His eyes got very big and said, "Oh, that means that Daddy can tell me a *cuentito* (a short story) every night now?". I tucked my kids into bed every night that I could and told them a *cuentito* before going to my corner to study till the late hours in the night.

Celebrating with my wife and children after the California State Bar Swearing-In Ceremony.

In essence, the whole experience of studying for the BAR exam had caused a high degree of tension and stress on me and on my family. I was feeling that perhaps my children resented my schooling and failed to understand why I had tried so hard and was unable to pass the exam. In this moment of celebration that belonged to all of us, I realized that the entire experience, including those two long months of separation from the family, was worthwhile. Now I was able to provide for my family who had stood by my side, supporting all my efforts. I also realized that I had never taken off more than a week or so from any of my responsibilities at work or at home to focus on the Bar Exam. This endeavor had truly been a family affair. It goes without saying that a united family will never be defeated.

"Success is not final, failure is not fatal, it is the courage to continue that counts."

Winston Churchill –
Prime Minister United Kingdom –
1940-1945, 1951-1955

LESSONS LEARNED

- The more you fail, the closer you get to success.

- Your family is the primary source of your moral fortitude.

- Every challenge in your life opens up another door to opportunity.

CHAPTER 12

The American Criminal Justice System - Case in Point

As I studied for the California BAR exam, I realized that I was becoming more knowledgeable of the law through studying for the BAR exam than what I learned in law school. I also realized that my approach to taking the BAR exam was merely different. When I passed the exam, I felt that I was the same person that I was before passing it. The difference was that I had opened the door to the future now that I could practice law, realizing a childhood dream, not only for me and my family, but for the community that I wanted to serve. Passing the BAR exam did not make me a smarter individual; it only gave me permission to practice law.

Instead of leaving my personnel director job immediately, I took my time in selecting the place where I was going to be employed as an attorney. I knew that I needed to work for an organization that would give me the opportunity to practice law through litigation. To me, litigation meant pursuing a legal matter through a process that potentially ends in a trial court, so I decided to seek a job at the Public Defender's Office in Fresno County, eventually earning a job there in 1981. My primary intent was to work in the Public Defender's Office for about six months, learning to practice law and gaining actual trial court experience. I always felt that I would be the one representing the underdog, the accused, or the David in a David vs. Goliath scenario. The six months of my intended tenure in the Public Defender Officer eventually became twenty-five years of law practice in the criminal justice system working as a criminal defense attorney and as an administrator.

The American criminal justice system is basically a conveyor in which justice is supposedly dispensed under the premise that there is justice for all; however, as I later found out, the administration of criminal justice in this country systematically revolves around a world of law, socio-economics, and politics where the wealthy become wealthier and many of the poor and many people of color go to prison. I recognize that this provocative statement appears to be an oversimplification, but it actually is a conclusion that I began to reach while I was practicing law as a deputy public defender.

I started to see myself in the faces of the people that I represented. I began to see clients that looked like me and like some members of my extended family and like some of my friends. I began to strongly identify with the accused, while having reassured myself that I had been very fortunate in my life in not having the misfortune of becoming the accused in this system of criminal justice. I had never committed an act which could be construed to be a crime under the law, although I was involved in situations, pranks if you will, that could have resulted in my being accused of a criminal act which would have been enough to provoke an extremely harsh punishment from this system that now seemed to me to be so intolerant of people of color and people that are poor.

In time, I realized that the punitive approach used by criminal justice courts was the very antithesis of what I had believed to be the rehabilitation ideals of a just legal system. I am not suggesting that my clients were all innocent, but rather that I felt it imperative that the indigent accused were to be provided with all fundamental constitutional rights by the rule of law. I soon realized the harsh reality of it all. How naive I had been to think otherwise. For example, a judge had made what I had considered to be a cynical but fairly accurate remark. He simply said, "Mr. Villarreal, this is a court of law, not a court of justice". As it turned out, this unexpected remark motivated me to be even more engaging in and out of the court system, seeking social and criminal justice, perhaps a la Don Quixote, seeking the impossible dream, nonetheless hoping that Lady Justice would not be illusory in my search for justice.

There were many instances when I recognized that my clients were guilty or were going to be found guilty, and they were going to be punished accordingly. There were also many instances where I thought my clients happened to be at the wrong place at the wrong time with the wrong people. I quickly learned how to make distinctions between process and merit. Learning how to navigate through the criminal justice system was just as important as considering the actual merits of the case. Once again, I recognized the old adage that "those who control the process control the outcome". During my tenure at the Fresno County Public Defender's Office, I found this to be the case.

I concluded that there were few instances of actual justice during my experiences in Fresno County in the state of California. At times, in this particular justice court system, I experienced subjectivity, racial animus, and even malice aforethought by officers of the court. On the other hand, I also learned that the process can work for you if you navigate it correctly. Persistence sometimes paid off, while at other times I would run into judges, prosecutors, and probation officers who refused to allow my clients to escape the arms of law enforcement by denying bail because my clients were poor and not because they were going to flee or were considered to be safety risks to the local community.

Using the analogy of baseball, it appeared that it was always that we, as criminal defense attorneys, were up to bat at the bottom of the ninth inning, with two outs, two strikes, and we were losing nine to zero. That's how I came to recognize the value of all of the knowledge that I had obtained in human relations, negotiation, communication, and conflict resolution processes that I learned in my previous jobs. I also recognized that my relevant life experiences were extremely helpful. The law was significant and so was legal procedure, but as I stood in front of judges and juries, and I presented my cases from a human perspective, I found this to be the most effective way to influence the people who wanted to see justice done. I then realized that the common bond was, and still is, the fact that we are all human beings and before the law we are, or should be, all equal. However, some political power players in the criminal justice system still believed that "we are all equal, but some of us are more equal than others".

As part of my criminal defense attorney routine, I was assigned to represent clients in Justice Courts, as they were known during that time, in the small rural towns in Fresno County. Every one of these towns was different in terms of the social, economic, and political culture. In one of these communities, the Justice Court was open only one day out of the week. The judge that presided over the court, to my unpleasant surprise, was treating our clients in a way that I felt was not only disrespectful, but racist as well. What was most striking to me was the way in which he referred to my clients vocally and on the court record as "wetbacks". On a weekly basis, he would give lectures on the record on how these "wetbacks", that appeared before the court, needed to learn how to follow the laws of this country and be good residents, all the while using derogatory terms such as "lazy" and "welfare recipients".

The first time I witnessed the judge doing this, I immediately asked for a recess during the proceedings and asked the judge to confer for a few minutes in his chambers. In chambers I asked the judge whether he understood the meaning of the term "wetback" in terms of connotation and how disparaging and offensive this word was. While speaking to the judge, it was clear to me that he failed to understand why I was asking him about the term. While being deliberately short and dismissive, he responded that he knew what the term meant. The following week, the judge continued to refer to my clients as "wetbacks" and once again I requested the judge for a recess. This time, he simply told me that I didn't understand his methods. In my short experience in the criminal justice system, I had not witnessed a judge operating along these undignified and offensive lines.

The next time that the judge used the term "wetbacks" in reference to the Mexican clients that I represented, I confronted the judge and he responded by saying "Jose, you don't understand, I would never call *you* a wetback". I decided at that moment to challenge the judge formally. In the court system of California, there is a commission that is referred to as the Commission on Judicial Performance, a state body that receives and investigates complaints against judges, and takes corrective action, if necessary. I decided to file a complaint against this judge to the Commission. I proceeded to seek the advice of individuals such as the prosecutor who was actually prosecuting my clients in this particular court. The prosecutor agreed to be a witness if and when I filed a formal complaint against the judge. I requested the Commission to investigate the allegation that this judge was using offensive and racist statements in his courtroom against my clients.

A few months later, after the Commission had investigated the case, the commission concluded that my complaint was justifiable. The Commission served the judge with a letter of reprimand, directing him to refrain from using the term "wetback" in court proceedings. Upon my returning to the court to represent clients in that Justice Court, the judge asked me to go to his chambers. He angrily said to me that I had destroyed his professional future, adding that I had wrongfully accused him of allegations that he claimed to be untrue. We both knew that as a result of getting this letter of reprimand, his chances of being considered for a higher court position would be minimal. The judge was furious. He looked at me with such anger in his eyes and demanded that I recognize his position. I told him in very clear terms that I understood and finished the conversation by saying, "Judge, you do what you have to do, and I'll do what I have to do". I felt that justice had been served. The judge refrained from using the term, at least in my presence, for the rest of the time that I represented my clients in his court. The judge became more respectful towards me and my clients. I realized then that sometimes one has to seek and find the moral fortitude to take a stand in situations where human dignity is being attacked.

On one occasion, while I was representing juveniles in the Fresno County Juvenile Court, I had the opportunity to observe what I considered to be racially based double-standard practices in the criminal justice system. On that particular day, I had two cases that were almost identical in terms of the facts of the case. I shall refer to these clients as "Johnny" and "Juan", since juvenile cases are confidential. While Juan appeared in court without his parents, they were working (parents are not required to attend), Johnny appeared in court accompanied by his parents, a family doctor, complete with letters of recommendation and other prepared materials. Johnny was white, Juan was Latino. Johnny and Juan were the same age.

When it came time to rule on the cases for official court records, the judge stated that Johnny would be released to the custody of his parents, given that it appeared to the court that he, Johnny, seemed to have characteristics that had potential for leadership in the community. The court indicated that Johnny would be released immediately. The court went through the same process of reviewing Juan's case, which included my request for consideration of Juan's release. The court stated that Juan had shown disrespect to the court, confusing me in the process for I had not witnessed any evidence of conduct that constituted disrespect. The judge ruled that Juan would be kept for thirty days in order for the court to consider rehabilitation options. I had argued that there was nothing negative about Juan's case, adding that, according to

Juan's probation file, he was doing well in school, his parents were doing well in supervising him, and that there were no major problems in the family at the present time. I was astonished and shocked by the decision of the Juvenile Court Judge.

During a recess that the judge had declared, I approached the judge in his chambers and stated to the judge, "With all due respect, your Honor, I have a statement and a question. These two cases are almost identical in every respect and yet, you released Johnny but not Juan, why are you doing this?" Additionally, I argued that based on race and financial status, it appeared to me that Juan was discriminated against. The judge looked back at me with discontent, and said in a stern manner, "Jose, this is the way it is". With that response, coupled with the visual discomfort expressed through his dismissive demeanor, it was clear to me that the judge was angry at me for even suggesting that his decision was based on economics or prejudice. Thinking that the judge would most likely punish other of my clients for what I had just done, I regrettably decided not to push the issue further with this particular judge because I would be taking cases before him often in the future.

On yet another occasion, I dealt with a case of a thirteen-year old Latino young man who was threatened with incarceration for refusing to attend school. Although this minor was not a delinquent, he had been officially declared to be a truant for not attending school. I had taken the case because I felt very strongly that being punished with incarceration for simply not going to school was far too harsh of a punishment. Although the case appeared to be routine, I eventually appealed the case to the California Court of Appeal and the California State Supreme Court. It turned out to be a very serious case where the California Supreme Court established that the California courts had the power to incarcerate a child, even if the child was not a delinquent.

At the age of thirteen, the young boy did not know how to read. The school district wanted to make a point in incarcerating him so that the school districts throughout the state could ensure that children attend school. I felt that even if the court had the power to incarcerate the child, the responsibility belonged to the school district, the parents, the family, and other institutions that basically failed to properly educate this particular child. The California State Supreme Court agreed that the court had the power to incarcerate the youth, but noted that the action taken, incarceration of the juvenile, should have been a last resort type of option rather than a first option. The State Supreme Court laid out a process which called for assistance for the child by the parents, teachers, court, and anyone that had anything to do with the education of a child, before they could consider the minor to be incarcerated. The circumstances had to be egregious for the courts to consider incarcerating the truant minor.

While we lost the case on the legal issue regarding the power of the court to incarcerate the youth, the fact that the court established a very stringent process that had to be followed before a juvenile could be incarcerated for not attending school was good enough to constitute a moral victory for those of us that believed that juveniles should not be incarcerated for not attending school. While the above-mentioned cases may seem to be inconsequential, the totality of the cases is illustrative of a pattern of prejudicial behavior that exists in the criminal justice system that can be construed to be detrimental to people that are poor or people of color.

As a criminal defense lawyer, I started to recognize that my clients, the criminally accused, were just as human as the rest of us in this world. They had the same ambitions, the same needs, and the same dreams as everyone else. However, I also realized that my clients were being treated very differently by the criminal justice system because of the numerous modifiable factors in their lives such as ethnicity, cultural background, and economics. As a result, these human beings were marginalized and demonized by a generally intolerant society that, even though these criminally accused appear to be equal before the law as dictated by the federal constitution, they were not treated as being equal before the law. The notion that you are innocent until proven guilty is almost immediately thrown out the window by those that control the process, leaving the criminal defense attorney as the last hope of constitutional protection for the accused. It is at this point in the process that the accused has to learn how to navigate the criminal justice system or face dramatic, costly, and dire consequences. Very few of the criminally accused are able to escape this harsh reality.

These observations in my early years as a deputy public defender, coupled with my own life experiences as an immigrant, motivated me to continue to practice law within the criminal justice system. At this point in my professional life I had gained experience as an administrative assistant, a human relations officer, a personnel director, a business owner, and an attorney. In addition, I had actively participated in civic community organizations. Given this over-all experience that I had obtained, I felt ready to take on a challenge as leader of a law organization. For these reasons, I decided to apply to become the Public Defender of Fresno County, a sixty-lawyer law organization of highly competent attorneys.

After six years of experience at the Public Defender's Office as a deputy public defender, I was appointed by the County Board of Supervisors to be the Public Defender due to, I believe, my professional experience in life that proved very valuable in running an office of 100 plus lawyers, investigators, and secretarial staff, fully dedicated to providing criminal defense services to the indigent accused. What started out as a negative experience as a deputy public defender turned out to be a very gratifying experience. I gained an opportunity to make the necessary administrative changes and ensure that our clients were properly represented throughout the criminal justice system.

In the meantime, I was participating in activities that were considered to be community-orientated, relating to non-profit organizations that repre-sented the poor, organizations such as the National Hispanic Scholarship Fund. These organizations were trying to enhance opportunities for both the poor and minority communities. While doing more work with the poor, I eventually learned to be culturally competent. I learned to understand the culture of the poor, not only from my own perspective as it related to my own experiences in both Mexico and the USA, but from the perspective of real people who find themselves trapped in the cycle of poverty. I learned to under-stand that being poor is not a state of mind when you are barely able to survive.

In the case of the indigent accused in the criminal justice system, if you are poor and innocent of the charges filed against you (being at the wrong place, at the wrong time, with the wrong people), the odds are simply against you if you believe that you will not pay any consequences. You will, most likely, be detained pending trial, you will most likely lose your job if you have one, and your name will be forever archived in the criminal justice system. This is your reality within the life cycle of poverty. Can you get out of this cycle? Maybe. You have needs and somebody has to be sensitive to those needs. You have to be respected and somebody has to show you that respect. You need someone that is culturally competent. To be culturally competent means being able to understand the person or group that you serve, it means being sensitive to the needs of others and most importantly, it means being respectful to others as human beings. In the Public Defender's Office, I learned to be culturally competent.

As the head of the Public Defender's Office, I found myself with a larger responsibility towards the community in which I lived. I was looked upon as one of the leaders of the community, and was frequently asked to participate in conflict resolution situations that pertained to organizations such as the chamber of commerce, social community organizations, and was even invited to be an adjunct professor at Fresno State University to teach Latino Leadership and Criminal Law. I found myself in a very gratifying position, engaged in a proactive stance in the future of my community.

At the same time, I had noticed that when the spotlight focused on me, I began to make enemies as well as friends. I realized that this came with the territory. Even some of my clients would turn on me due to the fact that my name was well known. Some of my clients felt that I had not done my job as well as they had expected it to be, and I was subjected to many physical threats made by both former and present clients. I received messages that threatened the well-being of both myself and my family. I felt uncomfortable, but at the same time I felt that these were necessary risks of my job. At one point in time, the county sheriff's office suggested that I consider applying for a permit to carry a weapon for my own protection and the protection of my family. My response was simple: "When I have to carry a weapon to do this job, it will be time for me to leave the job". I never applied for a permit to carry a weapon.

As the chief administrator in the Fresno County Public Defender's Office, I was in charge of supervising around sixty lawyers and support staff. When I applied for the position of County Public Defender, after having been in the office for a mere six years, my colleagues were all surprised and felt that I had not been there long enough to be qualified for the position. I felt that I had not only the experience and the required skills, but also the administrative knowledge needed to successfully manage such an important office. Supervising attorneys, in general, is a big challenge. Some have said that supervising attorneys is like herding cats. Attorneys are independent and egocentric. Moreover, criminal defense attorneys, by nature, are very aggressive.

As I was navigating the process of applying and competing for the lead position, I sensed that there were groupings of lawyers, judges, and political figures inside and outside the criminal justice system that did not want someone like me to attain the position. The undercurrent commentary in this process was that I was an outsider in what was now considered to be a traditional office of attorneys in the eyes of the local legal community.

During my tenure as Public Defender, I felt that I had made proper changes in the areas of affirmative action and diversity, because I hired many new attorneys that were members of minority communities and women. The present Public Defender is someone that I hired twenty-five years ago. During the same tenure, there were many instances where I engaged in the Fresno County criminal justice system in trying to modify the system's position against the indigent accused. I felt that I failed to make significant changes, but at the same time, I felt that some Fresno County officials had finally recognized that the indigent accused have a constitutional right to be adequately represented in the criminal justice system, just as well as anybody else does.

Having seen numerous cases come through in which the clients were young, yet bright enough to be rehabilitated, I often ran into former clients in public settings who would walk up to me and say, "Thank you for the representation. I am now working and raising a family". These moments made me extremely proud to have served as a criminal defense attorney. On the other hand, many clients were cynical about the system. I remember very clearly a former client of mine, a fifteen-year old mother of three, who had asked me whether I was a fool or just plain stupid for suggesting that she obtain a job at McDonalds. Her reasoning was that she could make five hundred dollars a night carrying a "bag of goodies", as a drug mule, and that I was very naïve to think that a fast food restaurant would provide anything of value to her and her family.

These and other relevant experiences, as the Fresno County Public Defender, offered me a clear picture of Fresno County, its residents, and its culture in the area of social and criminal justice. The work in this office was clearly challenging, but highly gratifying.

LESSONS LEARNED

- We must advocate for justice because injustice anywhere is a threat to justice everywhere.

- Justice should never be dispensed depending on the color of your skin or on the basis of your wealth.

CHAPTER 13

How to Survive a Traffic Stop

Being a criminal defense attorney can be intimidating. Within my role in the criminal justice system as a defense attorney, I had to deal with, not only with my clients, but with prosecutors, probation officers, law enforcement officers, and of course, judges, but I never thought that I would ever deal with a situation where I would be suspected of having committed a crime. Now, *that* can be intimidating.

The most memorable occasion where I found myself in such a situation happened while I was working at the Juvenile Detention Center in Fresno representing youth who were charged with criminal offenses. One day my car broke down and the mechanic said that it would take about two weeks to fix it. While my car was in the repair shop, my brother-law, Rolando, agreed to lend his car to me for a couple of weeks. He had a Chevy lowrider type of a car that was in good condition and it was his pride and joy. A lowrider car is a vehicle that has been modified so that its ground clearance is less than its design specification. The lowrider is sometimes identified with Latino gangs, but it is also can be considered to be a classic car. During the course of those two weeks, I was stopped on three different occasions in an area close to the Juvenile Detention Center, located in the *barrio* of southeast Fresno, California. I had heard and read about "racial profiling" and "driving while brown", but I had never experienced it myself.

On the first day that I drove the borrowed lowrider car, I was stopped by a police officer about two blocks from where I was working at the time. I remember rolling down my window and asking respectfully, "Good morning, what is wrong, Officer?". The first step in dealing with police officers in this type of circumstance, as I had been told before, is to be respectful. The officer replied, "What are you doing in this area?", he asked in a suspicious manner. I explained that I was working as an attorney at the juvenile center, a story that should not have been be too hard to believe considering the fact that I was wearing an attorney's uniform (a suit and tie) and possessed proper identification at the time of the traffic stop. The officer proceeded to tell me that I was driving a car that looked suspicious. "What?", I asked. The officer's tone became very aggressive as he began to question me. I then said, "With all due respect, Officer, I do not understand why I was stopped, nor do I understand why I am being questioned". He then asked me in a very belligerent manner where I worked, where I was coming from, and where I was going. He then asked for specific details, pertaining to documentation reference to my line of work. Satisfied with my responses, the officer simply said, "Move on".

I was able to survive this particular stop by following four basic recommended steps for this type of situation. Following are the four basic recommendations.

1. **Be Compliant, Respectful, but Observant.**

Pay attention to names, badge numbers, and requests that the officer is making. However, while you are making these observations, refrain from making any comments that may be construed to be confrontational or defiant. This will only serve to anger the officer and portray possible belligerence on your part which will be recorded in any report that he/she may fill out as a result of the stop.

2. **Watch Your Proximity and Keep Your Hands Visible.**

Refrain from getting too close to the officer, making hand gestures, or otherwise coming close to touching the officer in anyway. Even a mere hand gesture can provoke the officer to respond with physical action against you. Do not make any attempt to get your wallet or to get to the glove compartment. On this note, any defensive behavior on the part of the citizen, during *any* occasion, may provoke conflicts between the officer and the citizen. Moreover, any touching by you on the officer may be construed as a battery, an assault, or as resisting arrest. In other words, as my experience as criminal defense attorney has shown, a routine traffic stop may result in a misdemeanor, or even more serious, a felony. Without question, the consequences on this type of situation can be very serious. Remember, always keep your distance from the officer(s).

3. Do Not Project an Attitude of Confrontational Defiance.

The basic approach in a traffic stop: be respectful, cordial, and compliant. If the officer asks for a license and you don't have one, tell the truth in a non-defensive way. They will find out the truth either way, and being honest will help the situation become a smoother process. Nowadays, the officers do not have the right to take information from your cellular phone. However, the officers have the ability of recording whatever happens during the interaction. They may use any sign of your defiance as evidence to incriminate you at a future time. Exercise your right to remain silent. Don't ever think that the more you say, the more reasonable the outcome will be. An officer's main goal during any stop is to control the situation. Don't make comments such as: "I'm in a hurry, Sir" or "I'm late for work," which will only serve to interrupt their ability to control the situation. Remember, you happen to be part of the situation that the officer is trying to control. Always be aware of your own tone while addressing the officer in any manner.

4. Know Your Constitutional Rights

In order to exercise your constitutional rights, you must know what those rights are. Law enforcement officers do not have to read or tell you what your rights are but you can exercise your rights. You never know what you may have in your car's glove compartment or trunk, so you should not voluntarily consent to the search of your vehicle. Any relevant legal issues may be handled at a future time.

Follow these rules and you should be able to handle the traffic stop. By the way, the above suggested steps to be taken in a traffic stop are not mine originally. These suggestions are usually offered in traffic school settings. I offer the advice simply because of its practicality.

The second time I was stopped, within two weeks of the first time, in the same area by a law enforcement officer, I was asked many of the same questions that the previous officer had asked. Law enforcement officials have a tendency of being fast-paced, suspicious, and ready to control the situation. As the previous officer did, the second officer told me to leave the area as soon as possible, and to refrain from driving that style of vehicle again, if at all possible.

The third time an officer stopped me, again, within the same two weeks, the officer actually explained why he had stopped me, admitting that he had made a mistake. He also admitted that he may have asked more questions than he should have, though I do not recall a specific apology. Nonetheless, all three officers used similar methods of racial profiling based on the vehicle I was driving and the color of my skin. Profiling has continued and will continue to exist. It is a reality that Americans, specifically people of color who are poor, will regularly deal with these uncomfortable but potentially dangerous situations during routine traffic stops. After these three traffic stops, while driving a lowrider type of car, I finally got my car from the shop. Although I drove the same route daily to and from work for two and a half years after the three traffic stops, I was never stopped again in that particular vicinity by an enforcement officer. I can only wonder whether these three traffic stops were ever officially recorded. What I don't wonder about is the chilling effect that these traffic stops had on me.

Given the present state of immigration enforcement in this country that is based on a strong Trump-like anti-immigrant sentiment, it becomes imperative for you and me to explore different strategies to use when we, as people of color, immigrants, both undocumented and documented, are driving and are stopped on a suspicion of a mere minor traffic violation. We must anticipate almost every possible consequence that may land us in harm's way. What does all this mean? It means that you and I should carry with us every document that will clarify our immigration status, past, present, and future, period. A state granted Identification Card with a picture such as a valid driver's license may do. In addition, we should be ready to present documents that will explain our temporary status in this country, for example a work visa or tourist visa.

Finally, we must know and be ready to exercise all of our constitutional rights under these circumstances. We must remember and emphasize that even undocumented immigrants have constitutional rights. To ignore the above practical advice may certainly result in possible detention, arrest, and deportation. Please be aware that this is not an exaggeration. This is simply a reality that we as immigrants are living now in this the greatest country in the world. While this may sound a bit sarcastic, it is true.

LESSONS LEARNED

- Racial profiling has had a chilling effect on our every-day driving.

- On a traffic stop situation, you as the driver must be respectful of the officer stopping you, but be cognizant of your constitutional rights.

- Do not act foolishly in a most important traffic stop moment!

CHAPTER 14

Professional Experiences as Administrator

My professional experience as the Fresno County Public Defender produced good results. My administrative skills improved to a point where I felt confident in facing the daily administrative challenges of the job with a high degree of effectiveness. My legal knowledge was improving continuously. Without question, I recognized that there were many attorneys that knew much more than I did when it came to criminal law and procedure, but I also recognized that part of my job was to hire, train, and retain top-notch criminal defense attorneys who would provide the best criminal defense services to our indigent clients. In addition to increasing my administrative and legal knowledge, I learned to navigate the political environment of the Fresno County criminal justice system. During my eight-year tenure as County Public Defender, I managed to build a substantial tool box that helped me in the next stage of my professional career. After those eight years, I realized that it was time for me to move on to other professional challenges.

Throughout the years, I maintained a connection with family and friends in the County of Santa Clara, which was sufficient enough to arouse my interest in transferring from Fresno County to Santa Clara County when the position of Public Defender of Santa Clara County became vacant in 1995. The Santa Clara County's Public Defender's Office had ample resources, a highly qualified staff of 100 plus attorneys, a support staff, and most importantly, a strong administration of justice policy support of the governing County Board of Supervisors. I always knew that Santa Clara County was a wealthy county with a solid policy in social and criminal justice. Generally, offices such as the Office of the Public Defender are administered by an official who is appointed by the County Board of Supervisors. It became very clear to me that this was indeed a political appointment and that I had to overcome process and political hurdles that seemed to be difficult to overcome. Nonetheless, this was the dream position that, at this point in my professional life, became a desirable goal for me to reach. After six months of navigating through the processes of application, screening, and political maneuvering by my supporters, I was appointed to be the Public Defender of Santa Clara County.

What I learned from this strenuous experience of jumping through the administrative and political hoops of the appointment procedures of this highly regarded position was that one can persevere with the proper attitude. I heard my father's words of guidance: "Life is not fair, but as long as you ignore the negative, look forward, don't do any harm to anyone, and do the best you can, you will eventually succeed". He was right.

Santa Clara County had a large pool of resources that allowed the Office of the Public Defender to serve the needs of the county residents. Most importantly, the county governing officials recognized the public value of providing legal services to the indigent accused. The office was solid when it came to the operational capacity needed to adequately represent the accused. In comparison, Fresno County had limited resources to adequately provide legal services and the governing officials were not all that supportive of providing legal services to the poor. However, the Fresno County Public Defender's Office staff had the heart and the soul to put forth the effort to provide the best possible legal representation to the indigent accused. Overall, in the ten years that I served as the County Public Defender in Santa Clara County, I applied all my efforts in providing adequate legal services to the indigent accused.

My employment experience in Santa Clara County clearly met my expectations of opportunities in the legal field. It was exceptional. My responsibilities as an administrator placed me in situations where I was constantly challenged to utilize all the skills that I had learned and developed during all aspects of my life, both personal and professional. I also relied on the life lessons that I learned in my youth in Mexico and as a young immigrant navigating throughout all the unique areas of the USA, both urban and rural. Adapting to unwanted change by moving from city to city, school to school, barely keeping up with different situations was draining but, at the same time, exhilarating. As an administrator I had to be not only an effective manager, but also a truly effective leader. Although my knowledge and experience in the political arena was sufficient to get me appointed to the post, I had to constantly improve my skills in this constantly changing arena in order to survive the constant challenges of the job.

The CRLA Experience

Three areas where I enhanced my professional capacity were community engagement, leadership development, and cultural competency. During my tenure as the Public Defender of Santa Clara County, I became very active in fighting for social justice. While working with Fresno County, I was asked to be a board member of the California Rural Legal Assistance Program (CRLA), a legal advocacy organization established in 1966 as part of President Lyndon Johnson's War on Poverty programs. The organization had immediately established itself as one the premiere legal powerhouses in the area of legal advocacy on behalf of the ethnic rural poor in the state of California.

Early legal impact successes included stopping the practice of placing non-English speaking children in classes for mentally disabled students. In addition to class action cases, CRLA provided, and continues to provide, legal services in other relevant areas. This legal justice organization came into existence at a time when it was greatly needed. CRLA opened numerous legal offices throughout rural California with the idea of having attorneys in each office that were responsive to the local legal needs of the working rural poor.

During the 1960's, the political situation in relation to the rights of farm workers was bleak; the working conditions for farm workers were unbearable. CRLA's goal was to ensure that agricultural workers in California were treated humanely as they went about their work, harvesting fruits and vegetables for American consumers, as well as the rest of the world. Having experienced life as a farm worker, I recognized that as a CRLA Board Member, I had an opportunity to improve the lives of farm workers throughout the state. As I joined this most noble effort as a Board Member, I began to participate actively in developing organizational policies that continued to result in litigation victories for farm workers in the improvement of their working conditions throughout the state of California.

Holding CRLA banner from left to right: José Padilla, Director of CRLA, my wife, Enriqueta, and myself with other Board Members participating in the funeral procession for Cesar E. Chavez (1993).

One of CRLA's most successful cases was referred to as the case of *El Cortito* (the short one). The term referred to a short hoe that the farm workers used to thin, weed, and extract certain crops. The length of the handle on the hoe was eighteen (18) inches. To use it effectively, the farm workers were required to stoop all day long in the fields, subjecting them to back pain and back injuries. The human body was simply not built to endure this position for long periods of time. The short hoe allowed for faster production, but the constant use of this particular hoe eventually negatively impacted the health of farm workers.

Assisting the efforts of the United Farm Workers Union, led by Cesar Chavez, CRLA proceeded to legally challenge the use of this type of hoe and was eventually successful. The courts determined that the use of *el cortito* was no longer legal. This was a big victory for CRLA and farmworkers around the state, who would no longer have to unnecessarily strain their backs through the use of these tools. From that point on, farm workers were allowed to use a longer hoe that did not damage their health and yet accomplish the same task. As members of the CRLA board, we always felt that we were serving justice, with all of our efforts usually resulting in valuable contributions to our farmworker community.

I served on the CRLA Board for more than twenty years, including six years as President of the Board. Eventually, after retirement, I served as a Deputy Director of Administration on a temporary basis and recently I conducted leadership training sessions for CRLA Board community representatives. My tenure with CRLA was certainly one of the most satisfying professional experiences of my life.

The Harvard Experience

Starting in 1999, and stretching periodically into 2005, I attended numerous executive leadership sessions at Harvard University at their School Center for Public Leadership, within the John F. Kennedy School of Government. My ultimate goal was to become a better administrator and a better leader in local county government. The John F. Kennedy School of Government had set up what Harvard refers to as an executive leadership program in which they offered leadership courses by inviting prospective students from public, non-profit, and private sectors. The principal goal of the Kennedy School of Government is to develop ways of approaching local community challenges with the ultimate goal of effectively training their executives and leaders to resolve problems in a concerted effort in their roles within the public, private, or non-profit sectors.

The program participants represented local communities throughout the country and places throughout the world. It has been said that Harvard University has a unique way of controlling the world through programs similar to the one I attended. The school brings you in, charges you or your organization thousands of dollars for participating in these executive programs, and makes sure that you actively participate in their leadership training classes to develop programs that will help you to resolve the social, economic, and political situations in your communities.

What I learned at the Harvard Kennedy School of Government was that I actually knew more than I thought I did, but at the same time, I did not know much of anything. As one student stated after attending one of these Harvard programs- "I am still confused, but at a higher level". This statement reminded me of the great Socrates when he said, "True wisdom comes to each of us when we realize how little we understand about life, ourselves, and the world around us."

After serving as County Public Defender of Santa Clara County for ten years, I felt that professionally I was ready to move on to the next stage in my life. Santa Clara County had been good to me and I felt that I had accomplished what I had set out to accomplish; that is, I had successfully administered a county legal services program that served the county residents well with efficient and effective legal representation to the indigent accused and, in doing so, I had done justice to my job the best way I could with the financial resources that I had. Now it was time to retire professionally.

LESSON LEARNED

- Knowledge is fundamental, but experience coupled with knowledge will open more doors of opportunity.

CHAPTER 15

Becoming Mayor of an American City

It has been said that retirement means not knowing what day of the week it is on any given day. I was also told that retirement meant finally being able to say "no" to people without fear of losing your job. I even removed my wristwatch as a symbolic gesture of retirement. Eventually, however, due to my status as a retired attorney administrator who had been involved in the City of Sanger community issues before, neighbors approached me to attend a neighborhood meeting in Sanger. I declined at first, but due to persistence by a group of concerned citizens, I agreed to attend a meeting in a private home to discuss the abundance of critical issues that were affecting the citizenry of the City of Sanger.

The residents of Sanger, a California city in constant political turmoil, were in dire need of citizens that would actively engage in the governance of the city. The city needed help in crucial areas such as economic growth, urban redevelopment, budget management, and crime reduction. After attending a few home meetings, I was persuaded to actively participate politically. Numerous Sanger residents had openly expressed that the Sanger mayor at that time and some of his cohorts were on a quest for power just for the sake of power and that they were making decisions that were not in the best interest of the Sanger community. It thus became imperative for all of us as residents of Sanger to work together and confront this damaging situation head on. My interest evolved to a point that I became interested in running for a position in the Sanger City Council.

A small group of Sanger residents started off by holding meetings to gather information and to strategize the way in which we would confront the mayor and his cohorts. Our citizen group began to raise concerns with all Sanger residents that would listen to us in order to prepare for the forthcoming elections. At first, I had no intention of running for office. I had made the comment at one point that if a particular person, whom I admired and thought to be highly qualified did not run for office, I would take his place as a candidate, for I felt qualified to serve as a member of the Sanger City Council.

In prior years, I had been a member of the Sanger Chamber of Commerce, as well as a member of the Planning Commission. I believed that this experience coupled with the fact that I was an attorney and had attended several Harvard John F. School of Government executive leadership training sessions clearly qualified me to be a member of the Sanger City Council. The group of concerned citizens and I set out to connect with other local concerned citizens, choosing citizens who were ready to put forth time, effort, and money, and other resources needed to be successful in the forthcoming elections of November 2008. People who we were choosing to participate had a high degree of integrity and interest in the issues that our group was addressing. We ended up with a very strong team, which included my son, Adrian, as my Campaign Manager, and my long-time neighbor, as Finance Manager. My neighbor and I were referred to as the Odd Couple, because our opposite political stances, he was conservative and I was liberal. The common ground between us was that we both believed in the efficient and effective governance of our city.

We connected successfully with perspective Sanger voters through practical and effective use of communication techniques, like going door to door, asking questions, conducting marketing campaigns, doing fundraisers and even setting up a website. As the election campaign picked up, the individual that I was running against, the Mayor pro temp, decided to withdraw from contention and I ended up running as the sole candidate for my district. As a result of the effective efforts of my family, neighbors, friends, and concerned citizens of Sanger, my election was successful. By becoming a member of the Sanger City Council, I had become partially responsible for the governance of a city that was in dire need of good, effective, transparent, and accountable governance. I knew that the need for reform was there. I just did not realize the magnitude of the work that would be necessary to carry out such reform.

On the night that I was sworn in as a new member of the five-member Sanger City Council, I became the new Mayor of the city of Sanger. My selection as Mayor by the other city council members was due mainly to the participation of concerned citizens who had attended the meeting and spoke on my behalf. The speakers cited my qualifications to take on the town's leadership; consequently, the council members voted me in as the mayor. My main responsibility from that point on was to lead a group of council members in the areas of effective policy-making. As I came into the picture as the Mayor of the City of Sanger, I knew that in order to be successful in leading this city council, it was necessary for the whole group to have the same goal. Unfortunately, that was not the case.

I had campaigned on the principles of transparency and accountability. Soon it became clear to me that my colleagues in this city council were not interested in open government nor were they interested in being held accountable by the citizenry that they were serving. Whatever happened to the idea that when you are elected to serve as a public official, you have a civic duty to openly govern with input from your constituents and with the focus on governing for the common good and, if you fail to do so, you should expect to be held accountable? What a noble idea.

As I began to serve as Mayor, I noticed that my colleagues on the city council were more interested in protecting their own personal interests rather than in protecting the interests of the community that they were obligated to serve. We simply did not a have a common goal. Leadership has been defined in many ways. I choose to define it as an on-going process of influence between the leader and his or her constituents with a common goal for the common good. I subscribe to this definition of leadership by Professor Ronald A. Heifetz who taught at the Kennedy School of Government. In this particular Sanger City Council, it became clear that my Council colleagues and I were not on the same page, not only on the common goal, but also on the approach of reaching that goal for the common good.

The city of Sanger, California is a relatively small city with an approximate population of twenty-five thousand residents located in the inland Central Valley of California, close to Fresno, California. Sanger has always been known for its potential more so than for its real wealth of resources. The city is surrounded by agricultural farms and light industry sites. It is officially known as the Nation's Christmas Tree City because of its proximity to Sequoia National Park where the Nation's Christmas Tree, also known as the General Grant Tree, is in the nearby beautiful Sierra Mountain Range. The great Kings River passes close by and sustains the water needs of the area. Fresno County roads and freeways surround the city to provide adequate access to and from the city to neighboring cities. Sanger has a Hispanic population of approximately eighty percent of which more than fifty percent are agricultural migrant workers.

In the last twenty years or so, the expanding population of neighboring cities such as Fresno and Clovis have made Sanger an attractive option for residency and this new development has brought new challenges to the city that really has great potential of becoming, not only a bedroom community, but a city of destination. The new challenges for the city consist of not only basic infrastructure problems but also of continuing seasonal unemployment, crime related activity, cultural inter-neighborhood relations conflicts, and economic development issues. These old and new challenges have put a serious strain on the not so strong governance of Sanger.

Whereas past community leaders used to govern the city with a provincial attitude of an agriculturally based world, the new generation of community leaders are transitioning into a new world of challenges in government that includes new methods of influence through high tech communication. Communities in small towns and cities in California, and in the whole country for that matter, historically used to rely principally on the editorial pages of the local paper to engage in public discourse regarding issues that affected the local community. The Sanger community was no exception. For the longest period of time, the local newspaper, *The Sanger Herald*, was considered to be the conscience of the city, almost entirely by self-designation on the part of the owner of the newspaper. The editorial section of the paper was, in essence, the chosen forum when it came to the public discourse of critical community issues. The city council was the principal governing body for final consideration and decision-making, but the editorial commentary of the *Sanger Herald* was the most influential in the decision-making process.

Soon after, *The Sanger Herald* was no longer the main forum for discussion of issues and its editorial influence began to diminish. The internet had arrived and with it came a new era of open civic engagement in local politics. However, the arrival of the internet did not necessarily result in better government. This new world is what I came into when I became Mayor of the City of Sanger.

My expectation, principally due to my political naïveté, was that my city council colleagues were receptive to working in concert with me towards the goal of developing reform policies in the areas of budget administration, ethical political behavior, and economic development. During the first meetings, I noticed how dysfunctional this governing body was in carrying out its responsibilities. The budget process was dismal at gathering information, project development, and budget presentation. At one point, I actually described the Sanger budget process as nothing less than a shell game. In the area of ethical behavior, some individual city council members saw themselves as having the authority to micromanage the city staff into carrying out certain duties for the council members' personal benefit. In the area of economic development, certain council members were allegedly asking for favors from housing developers in exchange for council member votes which would benefit the developers.

These and other similar allegations were so rampant that concerned citizens took it upon themselves to file complaints with the Fresno County Grand Jury hoping that the Grand Jury would conduct necessary investigations focusing on the allegations against certain city officials. The Grand Jury eventually finalized the relevant investigations and found generally that there were serious deficiencies in the governance of the City of Sanger. The Grand Jury offered a set of recommendations to correct the deficiencies and the city of Sanger agreed to take corrective action.

In the meantime, the city council proceeded in a defiant course that was not reflective of any intent to self-correct. I soon realized how my colleagues were using the closed sessions of the city council agenda to carry out an agenda which was, in essence, contrary to the interests of the Sanger citizenry. I reacted by simply refusing to participate at all in closed session meetings. I then asked the county district attorney to look into possible violations of state laws. The district attorney issued a letter supporting my position and directed the city council to comply with state laws. During this whole process, I felt frustrated that I had to force the council to change its ways towards better governance.

Things were getting better, but I was physically being affected by the political turmoil to a point where I began to have serious health issues, which eventually forced me to retire from my position as a member of the Sanger City Council, and therefore from my position of Mayor of the City of Sanger. I was now going to have to engage in another challenging battle. Despite the unfortunate health circumstances that ended my tenure as Mayor of the City of Sanger, I felt honored to have served as the Mayor of this community of so many good citizens.

LESSONS LEARNED

- Politics nowadays is no longer like playing chess or checkers. It is like playing pool. Most of the time, you do not really know what is going to happen.

- Politics and truth are like oil and water, they do not mix.

- When you are in government, you are in the business of government, not in the business of business.

- When you become a public servant, you must cease being a servant to yourself.

CHAPTER 16

Raising a Family as an Immigrant in the United States

Raising a family in the USA is not fun, but it can be. My wife and I raised four children that we dearly love. I am certain that we made many mistakes in raising our children, but as we reach the grandparent stage in our lives, we feel a high degree of comfort in having raised good kids that became good adults, loving parents, and without question, good citizens.

Since my wife and I never raised a child in a country other than the USA, I will not even attempt to compare different ways of raising a family in different countries. On the other hand, my wife and I did raise our children by navigating through the numerous and very challenging institutions that directly or indirectly impacted every one of our children as they were growing up. Early in our married life, we recognized that the immediate family, the church, the health system, the education system, the economic institutions, and the criminal justice system would impact the various formative stages of our children.

From the perspective of the Mexican immigrant parent, I believe that we sometimes wrongfully assume that this country provides an exceptional environment to raise a child. This country has a set of norms and customs that are in many ways ideal, but in many ways not. There are many variables included in this picture: economics, religion, tradition, culture, etc. These institutionalized factors impact the growth of a child either positively or negatively; therefore, we as parents must not only understand them, but we must be able to face them effectively in order to protect our children in their formative years. Our principal responsibility as parents must be to be fully engaged every step of the way.

To illustrate the point, let me describe a system with which I became fairly familiar when I was working as a criminal defense attorney in the Juvenile Court. This experience gave me an insight into a part of the American criminal justice system that, at times, dispenses equal justice in the treatment of minors but most of the time acts adversely to the interests of the minor. The fact is that most juvenile courts and juvenile detention centers in the United States are replete with minors that come from poverty or are members of minority groups or both, principally of African American or Latino background. This fact alone should give every parent pause as how the criminal justice system will apply justice to our sons and daughters. It thus becomes incumbent upon us as parents to educate ourselves, by whatever means, to a point of knowing how to raise our children with these institutions in mind. First of all, no newborn comes to this world with an owner's manual. Secondly, every child is different. Finally, we as parents have our own different ways of raising the child. The question then becomes, what is the most basic and effective formula to use in raising a child?

How to Raise a Child - The Five Basic Elements

During my employment tenure with Fresno County as a criminal defense attorney in the juvenile division of the Superior Court, I had an opportunity to expand my knowledge in the areas of child development and parenthood. Whether it was social science, child psychology, child psychiatry, or family law, it became imperative for me to use these disciplines in my daily dealings with minors, parents, and the courts.

As I continued to practice law in this area, I began to develop a formula consisting of elements necessary to raise a child so that the child would not show up in the Juvenile Court System. As I interacted with parents of the minors that I represented, I presented the parents with a brief basic formula that worked for my wife and I in raising our children. The five elements of the formula were: (1) love for the child, (2) care for the child, (3) proper discipline of the child, (4) involving the child in recreation activities, (5) involving the child in academics, and a bonus element: developing a cultural competency plan for the family. I indicated to the parents that if they incorporated these elements in raising their child, chances were that their child would not show up in "Juvie" as an accused juvenile delinquent. I would then briefly summarize each of the elements as follows:

1. **Parents must love their children.** A parent's love for their child is the basic foundation in raising a child. This positive emotional act is carried out by most parents almost by instinct, as a result of a biological bond that creates a strong attachment between parent and child.

2. **Parents must care for their children.** A parent must provide the child with whatever is necessary for the health, welfare, and protection of the child. A child depends on the parents for physical and mental health and safety.

3. **Parents must provide proper discipline to their children.** This may be the most challenging element for parents simply because discipline requires so much time and effort to carry out in an effective manner. Parents must make sure that a child fully understands and follows the basic rules of expected behavior for a child. Disciplining a child requires strong, fair, and consistent supervision by the parent. Do not coddle your child by over protecting them, accommodating them, or covering up for them. On the other hand, respect your child and do not abuse their fundamental rights. If the parents are not ready or willing to properly discipline their child, society will be ever so ready to use its own methods of discipline. I would not want my child to be subjected to the discipline practices of the Juvenile Criminal Justice system which has been considered in many circles to be a school for prospective criminals.

4. **Parents must ensure that their children are involved in recreational activities.** A child needs to be actively involved in daily individual or organized recreational activity to ensure necessary healthy body and mind development. Additionally,

it keeps the child out of trouble and it provides enjoyment to the family as a whole. Most importantly, children by nature need recreational activity as an outlet of or expression of excess energy.

5. **Parents must involve their children in academics.** School related activities are necessary to ensure the child's exposure to general knowledge and understanding as it relates to present and future development of the child. Education, both formal and informal, are necessary to excel in the development of the mind and spirit through learning. Parents need to ensure that their kids are doing their homework and are actively participating in school projects.

Bonus element: Parents must actively engage in these upbringing activities. Parents must put forth the time and effort in understanding the culture of child development in order to become sensitive to the daily needs of the child. Parent engagement requires more than presence. It requires active participation in their children's education at home or at school.

I recognize that the presentation of these five elements is rather simplistic, even over-simplistic, and without question it is easier said than done. On the other hand, I also recognize the value of formulas that are clear, precise, and concise. Given this recognition, I truly believe that applying these basic elements in raising children will result in beneficial outcomes to the child, the family, and to society in general.

As my wife and I became parents and started to raise a family, we tried to follow the most human way of raising a family. We asked numerous questions of friends and relatives, read books, paid attention to community customs, and applied principles and norms. We wanted to raise kids who were going to be free in expressing their feelings and making their own decisions as they went through transitions. In Eagle Pass and Piedras Negras, where my wife and I were born and raised, respectively, the family structure was somewhat unique because it incorporated both Mexican and American family values. We were expected to follow the Mexican tradition in an American setting or the American tradition in a Mexican setting. As often as possible, we tried to have meals together as a family, especially dinners. On Sundays, we followed the tradition that Sundays were reserved as family days. Family included our immediate family, grandparents and extended family. It always seemed to me that mothers made more effort than fathers to remain with family on Sundays.

One of the most important decisions that my wife and I made regarding our family was to move from a large city to a small town. Moving to a small town meant a smaller range of opportunities, but on the other hand, a small town provided us, as parents, an opportunity to have more control over the everyday influence that the living environment had on our children. We decided to move from the big city of San Jose to the small town of Sanger, California. Once we settled down in this small community, we were able to get to know our neighbors, the school environment, the local government officials, and business owners. We also had extended family in this small community. However, we never wanted to control our children using extreme measures that would hurt the child, physically or emotionally. My wife and I were frequently told that we were very fortunate to have good kids. We loved our kids, but we knew that the time, effort, and love, not to mention money, that we both invested in raising our children was the real reason why they turned out great.

Celebrating my wife's birthday with our kids and family, October 2004.

In trying to connect with relatives around the border towns, we attended family reunions, where we would exchange stories of our family ancestors. For example, I specifically recall the Villarreal family reunions in 1994 and 2004, held in Piedras Negras where I was born. Four-hundred people showed up from many cities in Mexico and various states in the USA. My wife's family, the Garza family, has held an annual reunion in California for more than twenty years now. We teach our children to embrace the value of family and relate to them stories of how their grandparents and great grandparents came from Mexico escaping from the revolution in Mexico in the early 1900's. Likewise, my wife and I, along with our children and grandchildren, have spent our own immediate family reunions with each other in Lake Tahoe, California every year. As a Latino family, we constantly give reference to our rich cultural history. We do it at the dinner table, through photo albums, books, videos, and dinner discussions. We feel it is important to celebrate our family's history. We constantly ask our immediate and extended family to come and partake in drink, food and celebration at family gatherings, holidays, and birthdays. Our family celebrations are culturally festive and full of pride. I consider my immediate and extended family to be truly bicultural and bilingual in every respect.

My wife and I with our eight grandchildren in our backyard, 2019.

Together, we raised our four children: Rolando, Meliza, Adrian, and Alejandro, all of whom were raised with family values as we defined them. We loved our kids, we provided shelter and food, and although our economic situation fluctuated wildly, we responded well to the needs of our children as they began to develop into young adults. For more than twenty years, after having provided resources for our children, we tried to attend every conference, meeting, and educational opportunity that was possible to ensure the highest quality of this experience for them. We also made every attempt to attend every game, and any other recreational activity that they participated in. Sometimes our children played at the same time at different locations and that meant we had to split up in order to make sure one of us was there for them. Tiring yes, but fun and rewarding when you saw a smiling face telling you that they were glad you were there. Looking back on our choices, we may not have pushed them as hard as other parents, refraining from forcing our children to complete every homework assignment and every chore. I can say one thing for sure: we made every possible effort to ensure that the five key elements I mentioned were met while raising our children. As parents, we loved our children, we cared for our children, we disciplined our children, we made sure that our children engaged in recreational activities, and we made sure that our children were academically inclined.

Our 50th Wedding Anniversary (February 2015) celebration with all our kids and grandkids, and our family continues to grow... (New addition July 4, 2015).

Now that our children are fully grown adults, we have the pride in knowing that every one of them grew to be successful in their own lives. Success is somewhat subjective in the eyes of a family, but in our family, we define it as a pursuit of happiness. Each of our four children are providing for their own children, establishing us as successful grandparents, and themselves as loving and caring parents. I feel a very strong bond with each one of my kids, all of whom are very different from one another. I respect each one of them for what they have accomplished and what they continue to accomplish. I feel very strongly that the respect is reciprocated for both myself and their mother. My wife and I feel that our children are a source of pride and that they will continue to be successful in navigating through this journey of life.

LESSONS LEARNED

- Embrace the knowledge and the wisdom of your elderly family members, for they have walked the path that you are about to walk.

- Raising a child in any country is like cooking. It requires you to use all ingredients according to taste, but you must not forget to use tender loving care.

- When raising a child, a parent must be culturally competent; that is, he or she must understand the culture of children, be sensitive to the needs of the child, and most of all, be respectful to the child.

CHAPTER 17

Leadership Tools

The leadership immigrant stories that I have related in this book have dealt with the realities that we as immigrants face when we confront new and different environments. As we navigate new territory, we have to consider the options that we have and choose the option that we consider to be the most practical one, given the circumstances before us. Immigrating into this country from any country means considering the reality of the unknown with all the challenges that come with it. It is about change. It is about how one adapts to change. Whether the change is dramatic or not, it will immediately alter one's environment and one must respond accordingly. We must, therefore, learn to use the most useful leadership tools to effectively navigate the highly challenging journey of personal change toward the American dream. These tools are the leadership tools that assisted me in my journey as an immigrant in this country.

When I discuss leadership concepts or tools as they relate to entering a new country, I draw from my personal experiences as an immigrant. The definition of the term leadership that I apply in writing this book is one that I have chosen to be the most relevant definition. Leadership has been defined in many ways. There are hundreds of books, maybe thousands, that have defined leadership as a position, as a skill, as a tool, or as a process. As I have indicated before, I subscribe to the definition that Professor Ronald A. Heifetz at the Harvard Kennedy School of Government uses to describe leadership as "an ongoing process of influence between the leader and his/her constituents, with a common goal". This definition applies to the self as well. Having chosen this definition, I am not suggesting that other definitions are better or worse. I just believe that this definition reflects my perspective based on my acquired knowledge and experience. The following seven leadership tools are of equal value.

1. Move from the Notion of Limitations to the Notion of Possibilities

As my family immigrated to this country in the early 1950's, we were almost immediately relegated to the lowest societal status. We immigrated to enhance our chances of improving the socio-economic status that we had more or less enjoyed in Mexico. However, I soon realized that this country was not going to be a good host to us or to anybody that looked similar to us. From a young age, I felt that there was no welcoming committee for immigrants, and my notion of limitations began to develop. I wanted to continue to speak Spanish but I was punished if I spoke Spanish in this country. I was told, "You are in America now". I wanted to be enrolled in the third grade or its equivalent, but they told me, "You have to start at pre-kinder because you do not speak, read, or write English".

During the period of time that I was attending public schools in the USA, there was no such thing as English as a Second Language programs. I wanted to do many things that I was told I could not do. I began to believe that there was an invisible wall - the wall that holds the "I want to, but I cannot" attitude that set the background to my struggles until I changed my perspective from *no puedo* (I can't) to *sí puedo* (I can). To me, these walls, limitations if you will, were almost insurmountable. It took me years to make up for lost time, but eventually, I overcame the walls and moved on to the notion of possibilities. When it happened, it was almost magical! Of course, it took time, effort, work, and a push from individuals that recognized my potential. The echo of my father's advice, *"Ignora lo negativo y sigue adelante"* ("Ignore the negative and move forward"), stayed with me as I continued to navigate my life as an immigrant in this country.

When someone indicated that I could not complete a task, I would respond by saying to myself, "Of course I can". Many times, I was ready to throw in the towel. The best example of this was the obstacle course that I overcame while trying to become an attorney. The result was that, in spite of my limitations, such as language deficiencies, emotional and cultural barriers, and financial status, I ended up becoming a lawyer administrator in charge of the Public Defender Offices in Fresno County and in Santa Clara County and eventually the mayor of Sanger, California. No one should accept the notion of limitations; the trap of thinking or being told by someone else, including teachers and counselors, that you cannot achieve whatever goals you set for yourself. Stay the course, do the work, and view the finish line as a possibility. Eventually, nothing will stop you from fulfilling your dreams. There is a saying in Spanish: *"No hay que llegar primero, pero hay que saber llegar"* ("You do not have to get there first, but you have to know how to get there"). In other words, you have to persist as you navigate the journey until you reach your dream, whatever your dream may be.

In life, you can view things from a negative standpoint, or you may choose to view things in a positive light. If you stay within the notion of limitations, you begin to close doors on yourself, creating self-imposed limitations for your goals. Recognizing that you have the spiritual fortitude to become successful will open these doors in order to move forward. This does not mean that you will not fail from time to time, as long as you recognize that failure is a good way of learning. Someone once said "The more you fail, the closer you get to success". Most founders of successful companies will tell you that they failed many times before they reached a point of success. The notion of possibilities will always triumph over the notion of limitations.

2. Learn to Adapt to Change

Adapting to change can be one of the most powerful leadership abilities that one can possess. Simply stated, change is a process of action that transforms one state into another. Change is constant. Every day we find ourselves facing change in time, place, society, events, technology, and most notably, within ourselves. Change has an effect on us as individuals as well as collectively. Events such as birth, death, marriage, and disease will change our lives dramatically. Normally, we do not like change because change can be very stressful. It causes us discomfort and sometimes it threatens our security and stability. We may even lose control and make mistakes as we face change.

Therefore, in order to maintain our strength, we must learn to properly adapt to change.

As I was growing up, both in Mexico and the United States, I was constantly facing change by switching schools, cities, and friends. At one point in time, I was even reluctant to embrace new friends because I felt that I would lose them eventually. As time progressed, I somehow surrendered to the reality that I needed to embrace change, along with its never-ending possibilities. As I was growing up, my parents would tell me that change was good and eventually I started to believe it.

Reflecting on what steps I took to adapt to change as I was navigating through the journey in both Mexico and the United States, I recognized the process that I went through in dealing and eventually accepting change. Change by definition is a process of transformation or modification. Change is also a process of variation and deviation. It has been said repeatedly that change is a process that almost all of us do not like and prefer to avoid. I was one of those that did not like change as I was growing up in Mexico and in the United States. I had no choice but to adapt.

How was I to deal with this constant traumatizing change of events, places, people and circumstances? Early in my childhood I began to wonder how I was going to respond to the set of situations that developed as our family moved from city to city, as I moved from school to school, making and losing friends along the way. This change thing was a constant set of traumatic temblors and I felt it. I became ill, constantly vomiting, having severe headaches and constantly crying. I was not a happy child.

As a youngster, at what age I do not remember clearly, I began to realize, through observation, that the primary source of this ever dramatic and traumatic change was the head of our immediate family, my father. Don't get me wrong; I loved and respected my father very much. My father was not only the main provider for the family, but the principal decision-maker. My mother, on the other hand, was the principal person in charge of the family support system. She was in charge of providing daily family support as my father was working out of the house. My mother was in charge of the cave and my father was the hunter. How these conjugal roles were agreed upon, or not, I never found out exactly. Before my mother passed away, she indicated that she simply took on the responsibility of providing the necessary support to my father who would bring home the bread and would decide where and how the bread would come. My father once indicated to me that he always wanted to provide financial stability to the family. This was the way my parents dealt with at least this portion of the changing situations that they had to endure.

The fact that my father's decisions were the main source of my pain became extremely important to me. Once I questioned my father as to why we moved so much, since I wanted to stop moving. My father responded by saying, "Mijo, life is not fair - we have to move so that we can do better. You, as my son, have to support my decision and ignore all the negative things that life brings and do the best you can without harming anyone, not even yourself." I began to recognize what my own reality was and how I had to find a way of adapting to it. Now I realize how much I appreciate my parents showing me how to use this most important tool of leadership.

Just as I realized that I had no control over the change that was taking place in the world of my immediate family, I began to recognize that I had no control on the change taking place in the outside world. This was astounding to me. The world outside of me was going to continue to change this reality. What I began to recognize was that I did have control over how I would respond to change. I had choices. I could do nothing and totally lose control of change, I could confront change in a defiant way or I could run away from it, the fight or flight choice. The other option was a more practical one: embrace the change and adapt to it. The first step would be to surrender to the reality facing me. Then, I would go through a process of controlling the situation, considering the limitations, but most importantly, the possibilities. This was a process of understanding and gathering of information. Lastly, I would develop a plan of action with anticipated results, making no assumptions, and recognizing the risks and possible consequences. Easier said than done, but doable. This is how I adapted to change as I was growing up in Mexico and in the United States of America.

As I moved through other stages of my life, I realized that embracing change was bringing me more benefits than consequences. Without actually knowing it, my parents gave me the gift of knowing how to adapt to new situations and environments. I continued to use these approaches throughout the rest of my life.

One of the best explanations of how to adapt to change is laid out in the book, *Unlock the Fear* written by Gail Caissy, Ed. D, a prominent consultant in education. Dr. Caissy presents and examines seven clear steps on how to adapt to significant change: Disbelief, Intellectual Acknowledgement, Emotional Reaction, Limbo, Transition, Emotional Acceptance, and Integration.

One of the most dramatic changes in my life occurred when my family moved to the city of Chicago in the early 1950's. As a nine-year old kid, I faced the daily fears of living in a huge city, enduring the extreme cold weather with no appropriate clothing, going to a school where no one spoke or cared to speak Spanish and a generally hostile environment. These were my realities that required adapting to change. After several months of trying to adapt to such a dramatic change, my family lost and Chicago won. My father chose the flight approach and moved on to seek better ground in close-by Michigan.

Back in 1995, I applied for the position of Public Defender of the County of Santa Clara in California. I had served as the Public Defender of the County of Fresno for eight years and thought that it was best for my wife and I to move to an organization that offered an opportunity to grow with better compensation and retirement benefits. Having reached the age of fifty and our children being out of school, my wife and I decided to look towards building a reserve that would provide us with an opportunity to enjoy our golden years.

I was very happy upon being appointed the head of the very prestigious Public Defender Office of Santa Clara. However, one of the requirements of the job was to complete a medical examination. As a result of this exam, I faced an entirely new form of change in the face of diabetes. My life was on track, and my wife and I were looking forward to the new possibilities that lay ahead of us. Within a few months, after my wife and I had learned more about diabetes, we started to accept the reality of having to deal with a disease that cannot be cured but can be controlled. This was the emotional acceptance part that, in many ways, we were working toward. As a result of this emotional acceptance, my wife and I started to take steps of exercising, eating healthy, paying attention to medications, and minimizing stress levels on a daily basis. It was not easy but after several years, we succeeded in controlling diabetes. Health concerns are in a sense, easier to adapt than other changes throughout life. Without a doubt, health concerns forced change upon me. However, in order to properly adapt to change, I had to change my attitude as well. I viewed my health challenges as a gift, something that finally forced me to view my body as fragile and susceptible to disease.

Change is a constant in a reality that one has to confront. It is imperative that one learns to adapt to it.

3. Become Culturally Competent

Although the concept of cultural competence has been around for decades or even centuries, it is now beginning to take hold as an important human relations concept in this country. Cultural competency programs are now being developed and used in areas such as immigration, health, education, administration of social services, and the administration of justice. The concept of cultural competence is based on the premise that all of us in this world would be better off if we better understand each other, are more sensitive to each other's needs, and are more respectful of one another. Although this explanation may be considered to be an oversimplification of a problem that transcends any ideology, it encompasses the sufficient basic elements to successfully navigate in the USA as an immigrant.

Throughout my life in this country, I have not stopped trying to understand Americans in terms of culture, history, core values, economics, language, and politics. At the same time, I have also been trying to understand the culture of Mexicans and other Latinos. I do emphasize the word *trying* simply because it is a never-ending process. One thing I do know is that I have benefitted tremendously from this process. It has always been said that if you know yourself, you will win half of your battles but, if you also know your enemy as you know yourself, you will win most of your battles. As an immigrant, your enemy is the unfamiliar environment that you are coming into as you cross the border into this country. It thus becomes imperative for you to enhance your ability to understand all that you can understand about the USA in terms of its culture, including language, history, and customs.

Trying to be sensitive to the needs of the people that I live with is very challenging. Throughout my life as an immigrant, I have been treated very well, very poorly, and sometimes even indifferently. However, I am still trying to be sensitive to the needs of my fellow human beings because this approach of treating others with a high degree of sensitivity to their needs has produced good results for me and for the people that I encounter.

The element known as respect in the area of cultural competence is the most challenging element of cultural competence to put into use. By definition, respect is a feeling of regard for the actual or perceived qualities of the one respected. It was Benito Juárez, President of Mexico and contemporary of President Lincoln, who once said, *"El respecto al derecho ajeno es la paz"* ("Respecting the rights of others is peace"). Understanding the implications of these famous words provides us with the necessary foundation of respect as a necessary element of cultural competence. In order to gain respect from others, we must acknowledge the good in others, to reject differences in race, and social position. The history of the USA, including the sixty plus years that I have lived in the country, has certainly, and unfortunately, not demonstrated a high degree of respect towards immigrants coming from Mexico or from other parts of Latin America. Given that fact, it is extremely difficult to be respectful when one senses that the feeling is not mutual. Nonetheless, we must take the high road and hope that our gestures of respect will be reciprocated. In my case, I found that my gestures of respect almost always resulted in mutual demonstrations of respect.

4. Be *Terco(a)*- Be Determined

The meaning of the Spanish word *terco* usually has a negative connotation. It can mean that you are stubborn. It can also mean that you are determined, which is a very positive connotation. My mother referred to me as being *terco* whenever she felt I was acting stubborn, obstinate, contrary, defiant, deviant, or opinionated. I would respond by giving reference to the word *terco* as meaning that I was actually determined, resolved, decisive, and otherwise driven. Simply put, if I had not been *terco* in my approach to life, both in Mexico and the United States, I would not be here today, feeling content with myself. As my father used to tell me, *"Mijo, la vida no es justa, ignora lo negativo, no le hagas daño a nadie, ni a tí mismo, y sigue adelante"* ("Son, life is not just, ignore the negative, do no harm to anyone, not even yourself, and move on"). In order to follow that *consejo,* (advice) I had to be *terco.* It was by pure determination that I not only survived my life in Mexico, but became a relatively successful person in this country as well.

As I was growing up in my native Mexico, I realized that I had not been dealt the best of hands. I had been a sickly child, although I do not know the specifics of my health condition for my mother never elaborated on it. Soon after my mother enrolled me in elementary school in the first-grade, I was sent home because the school administrators indicated that I had an extremely serious speech impairment. My self-esteem took a dive. The only reason why I was readmitted back to school was because my mother would not take "no" for an answer from the schools. She too was *terca*!

Attaining goals of mine or of my parents was always a challenge for me. I always seemed to be slower in reaching the goal line. Eventually I learned that, with more time and effort, being *terco* was going to take me closer to the finish line. Learning was never easy for me. I still do not understand how to take standardized tests. I still have difficulty in organizing my thoughts. Again, because I was *terco* enough, I managed to overcome the academic obstacles, no matter the difficulty of the subject matter. I do know one thing, and that is this, if I eventually successfully passed an exam as difficult as the California BAR Exam, anyone can do it.

Being defiant is another form of being *terco*. When I was practicing law as a criminal defense attorney in Fresno, California, working for the Public Defender's Office, I was assigned to Juvenile court to represent minors. After a few minutes of explanation to the client about what my role was in representing him/her, I proceeded to tell the minors how they were going to survive their stay in Juvie. I advised minors to learn to be properly defiant. First of all, I told the accused delinquent minors that it was okay to be defiant. I emphasized that there was nothing wrong with being defiant. As a matter of fact, I told the minors that some of the most successful people in the history of the world had been defiant, including Jesus. However, I advised the minors to learn exactly how to be defiant, what to be defiant about, and where and when to be defiant. Being defiant required being familiar with the Juvenile Court rules of conduct, including the rights of minors and the administrative appeals process. Only then could minors begin using the rules and winning as a result of using those rules. Most of my Juvenile Court clients were pleasantly surprised to hear what I was telling them. They would usually follow my advice and would actually come back at a later time to thank me. Even though court judges did not approve of my approach, I felt that everybody in the Juvenile Court system benefitted from my advice, and for that reason alone, I continued the practice. I even had kids coming back as adults to thank me and even indicated that they use the same approach in their life. Be *Terco*!

5. **Your Word Must Be Impeccable**

As I navigated as an immigrant in this country, I began to realize, just as I did in Mexico, that truth is the highest standard of leadership. I understood that if my word was impeccable, I would gain the personal freedom to seek and attain success. As I was growing up in Mexico, my parents, teachers, church officials, and other persons that I respected would always emphasize the value of my word. They would tell me, *"Tu palabra debe ser impecable"* ("Your word must be impeccable"). As a matter of fact, when you begin to search for guidance, books such as, *Los Cuatro Acuerdos (The Four Agreements)* written by Don Miguel Ruiz, will teach you to place great importance on your word. Ruiz states the very same idea. He refers to Toltec wisdom philosophy to simplify the commitment that we should speak with integrity, that we should say only what we mean, that we should not gossip. This occurs only when you decide to use your word *"sin pecado,"* or "without sin." I highly recommend this book for its emphasis on spiritual wisdom as it relates to truth.

While I navigated through various challenges in my life, I noticed that staying true to my word would come with a price. There was always be a price to pay after choosing the truth as the right choice. Whenever I was truthful, I was transparent. In essence, every time I was truthful, I took the risk of being subjected to criticism, abuse, and ridicule. But the fact remains, in a long-term context, taking the high road always pays dividends. First of all, telling lies meant omitting the truth, which became hard to keep track of in certain situations. As I grew older, the benefit of refraining from lies became more apparent. I gained the respect of my relatives, friends, and my community, a collective support system for my journey through life.

6. **Learn How to Resolve Conflicts**

Throughout my life I encountered situations where conflict existed almost on a daily basis and some of them had nothing to do with the fact that I was an immigrant. While growing up in Mexico, I frequently engaged in conflict, whether the conflict was within myself, with individuals, or society. Coming into this country, confronting situations of conflict were intensified by the mere fact that I was on new ground dealing with different people and different rules. As I began to grasp the tools that allowed me to deal with conflict, I also began to realize how significant these tools were to an immigrant in order to succeed in this country.

Without going into an academic or intellectual discussion of how to resolve conflict, it is important to recognize that resolution of conflicts is necessary for an immigrant who wants to take a functional role in this society. Traditionally, conflict has been considered to be a negative consequence of change. Whether conflict is seen as a battle of the minds, or a mere disagreement, is a matter of degree or perspective. Only recently have we recognized conflict as positive. It can be said that conflict can even be seen as an opportunity to develop possibilities.

As an immigrant, I found myself in situations of conflict that were considered to be classic types of conflicts: self versus self, individual versus individual, and individual versus society. All situations fell into any of these categories. In any of the types of conflicts, I found that I always had options in seeking a solution to the conflict situation. One of the first options that I chose was to avoid the conflict by not addressing it through conversations or conduct. Sometimes I would choose to accommodate the situation or the person(s) in an attempt to alleviate their conflict. Compromising was the third option I had at my disposal. This option seemed to satisfy some individuals. Sometimes I would confront the individual or I would consider collaborating with the individual. These options were chosen carefully based on the conflict situation, the individual, and the desired outcome. The following are five classic options for conflict resolution.

Avoidance (not dealing with the conflict) worked some of the time. I did not have the time or, simply stated, I did not want to deal with the conflict head on. Most of the time, avoidance did not work for me because it would never actually solve the conflict, just prolong it.

Accommodation (to give in) would build good relations with individuals, like giving a pacifier to a baby. However, accommodation is usually unsuccessful in resolving most conflicts. It merely allows individuals to take advantage of the situation, relinquishing your sense of control.

Confrontation (fighting for power) can resolve the conflict rather quickly, often times trading a quick solution for a long-term answer. A fist fight, for example, would not resolve the conflict because it failed to analyze the root of the conflict itself.

Compromise (give and take) is sometimes good but, in actuality, everybody would lose, because no one is completely satisfied. However, this may be the best option since both sides come away with something.

Collaboration (problem solving, sharing needs) would work most of the time. Everybody would win through mutual understanding and mutual respect.

My preferred method of conflict resolution was to find out who was involved in the situation, what interests were being protected, what needs were desired, and what outcomes would benefit all those involved. This process will eventually lead to collaboration. One thing to consider, do not try to resolve or go through the process of resolving a conflict if one or all the parties are hungry, angry, emotionally distressed, or tired. Stop and proceed at a later time. With this caveat, any of the options may work under given circumstances.

7. Good Leaders Must be Good Team Players

While I was studying for the California BAR exam in July 1980 in Sacramento, California, I was invited by my brother-in-law, Pedro Vargas and his wife to spend a Sunday afternoon at their home in the nearby city of Elk Grove, California. On our way to Elk Grove, as we drove through one particular neighborhood, Pedro, a Vietnam War veteran born in Eagle Pass, Texas, noticed smoke coming from the top of a residence. As we got closer to the house, we noticed that heavy smoke was emanating from the front door as well. No one seemed to be in the house at the time. The outside of the home, as well as the surrounding neighborhood, was completely quiet, and bare of any human activity. I didn't think that this was unusual since it was a Sunday afternoon in a residential area. Suddenly, by instinct, Pedro brought the car to a halt and said to me, "Let's go". He told his wife to stay in the car as we got off and sprinted across the street towards the house that was burning at an increasingly alarming rate, with flames now visible through some windows.

As we approached the burning house, it was quite apparent to me that Pedro was immediately ready to enter the residence with intention of fighting the fire and perhaps saving a life in the process. Pedro took the lead and I followed him hoping to provide any assistance necessary. Although I had absolutely no experience in dealing with fires, it was clear to me that my brother-in-law had ample Vietnam War-related experience in confronting life-threatening situations. This house fire was certainly a life-threatening situation, and Pedro moved with the necessary self-confidence, intensity, and determination. As we entered the home, crawling below the smoke line, I remember asking myself, "What the hell am I doing here?". Pedro had entered the house with the intent of saving a life without even knowing if there were occupants to save. His determination to put out the fire and possibly save someone he could not visibly see is what drove me to follow his leadership in this extremely perilous situation.

When we made it past the front door, which was open for whatever reason, we began shouting loud enough to make our presence known, while searching for anyone who might be inside the house. We went from room to room on our knees and sometimes stomachs, dealing with thick blankets of smoke blocking our vision. We eventually made our way to the main bedroom and found a couple (male and female) who appeared to be asleep or passed out. They were both lying on a single mattress on the floor completely naked. Pedro and I immediately noticed the strong scent of marijuana, concluding that these two individuals might be under the influence of stronger drugs as well. After checking their pulse, Pedro indicated that both individuals were still alive. Immediately, Pedro pointed to a nearby window facing the street and shouted, "Open it and yell for help!". As it turned out, a passerby was approaching the window from the lawn and yelled, "A fire truck is on its way". The man was ready to help us and did so promptly. In the smoke-filled bedroom, we were struggling to carry two almost lifeless naked bodies, but eventually, were able to pass the bodies one at a time out the window to the gentleman waiting outside the window.

Pedro Vargas, a Vietnam veteran from Eagle Pass, Texas

The firefighters arrived within five or ten minutes and took control of the fire scene in a professional way. The firefighters extinguished the fire while Pedro and I recovered from the smoke we had just inhaled. Pedro had shattered his eyeglasses during the incident, and we were both having trouble breathing. Suddenly, somebody frantically yelled there was a child still trapped inside the house. Pedro was ready to go inside the house again but was told that the child was actually safe at a neighbor's home. After giving us assistance, the paramedics placed the couple into the ambulance and drove off to the hospital.

A television news media crew had arrived and approached the gentleman who assisted us in pulling the couple from the house. Pedro and I quickly left the scene and walked back to our car across the street while the news media crew interviewed the man. This life saving hero seemed to soak up his fifteen minutes of television fame, answering the media's questions with a wide smile of satisfaction on his face. Regardless of the media attention on other individuals, it was Pedro's instinct, courage, and act of leadership that saved two lives. At the end of the day, Pedro and I were nonetheless very proud that we had actually saved a couple of lives on that Sunday afternoon, without even realizing that we could have lost our own life in the process.

What I realized that day was that I was a good team player for following Pedro's lead and working in concert with him. I also realized that the synergy or interaction between Pedro and I produced a better result than the sum of our separate actions. This experience helped me recognize that sometimes one has to defer or submit humbly to another person's superior knowledge and experience level in certain situations. This recognition of always being a good team player was extremely helpful to me in future real-life situations.

LESSONS LEARNED

- In order to lead others, you must learn to lead yourself.

- You cannot be a leader, or ask other people to follow you, unless you know how to follow.

- Adapting to change opens more doors than resisting change.

- Understanding others will enable you to be sensitive to their needs and be respectful of their views.

CONCLUSION

My sincerest hope is that the information in this book will be helpful to immigrants and to those that interact with immigrants. As I navigated as an immigrant in this country, I confronted many challenges that were unexpectedly daunting and certainly demoralizing. Sometimes, I found myself alone and in dire need of assistance. Most of the time I was strongly supported by relatives, friends, and by good human beings who were so willing to assist me. Almost every lesson that I learned was learned by doing, by observation, and especially by listening to individuals that I followed or admired. As a result, I have enjoyed life, I have found joy, and I have given joy to others for more than sixty years. My hope is that every immigrant, documented and undocumented, uses the tools presented in this book as he(she) realizes the American Dream.

Today, I am facing challenges that almost everyone faces with age - health issues. In my case, I am dealing with diabetes, heart problems, cancer, and other related health issues. However, thanks to my loving wife, my immediate family, my extended family, and many great friends, I am still surviving. I have enjoyed navigating this journey that we call life. I am truly blessed!

APPENDIX A

Fresno Bee Article Regarding the Author

January 9, 1995

The following excerpts are from *The Fresno Bee Newspaper* article written by **Alex Pulaski** and titled: ***Spirited tenacity and hard work propel public defender to top***. At the time the author had worked as the Fresno County Public Defender for eight years.

"**Legal eagle**. José Villarreal is a fighter who's committed to Hispanic and farmworker causes."

"Hard work and a hard head are José Villarreal's hallmarks. "Terco" – stubborn – his mother calls him in Spanish, and Villarreal, 50, credits that determination with boosting him to the top of his Fresno County department and keeping him there seven years later."

"I think he is one of those rare people who brings the office together rather than splitting it apart. Avila (Ralph) said."

138

Villareal: Lawyer says the court system

Continued from Page B1
traveled to California and other states for field work, always wintering in Texas.

They finally settled in the Santa Clara Valley, and he received a degree in Spanish from San Jose State University in 1968.

That was the start of a "crazy time," Villareal remembers. He was married, working for a legal aid society and later the city of San Jose, and started attending law school.

By the time he finished law school six years later, he and his wife, Enriqueta, had four children, Rolando, Meliza, Adrian and Alejandro.

All or nothing

For six more years, he butted his hard head against the bar exam. Couldn't pass it. Kept trying. Thought about giving up.

In the meantime he changed jobs several times, including a stint running the family restaurant in Sanger, where he still lives.

He decided to give the bar exam all or nothing, and took two months to study. He passed in 1980, and today tells people only that he took the test "between two and 100 times."

In 1981 he went to work for the Fresno County public defender's office as a staff lawyer.

Tough job

It's not a glamour job, working in the dark corridors and basement courtrooms of the courthouse, cutting deals for people who sometimes view a free lawyer as no lawyer at all.

The slings and arrows he got then for trying to protect the rights of accused criminals are the same he gets today: "How can you defend a person who has committed a crime?

"What do you do when you know your client is guilty? How can you sleep when you are making every effort to get these criminals out of jail?"

The answer is more complex, but Villareal said it boils down to

the idea that every person, regardless of economic station, is entitled to a defense.

When the office chief's job opened up in mid-1987, Villareal was a trial lawyer trying to leap over a couple of layers of supervisors to the top.

The knock on him was that he didn't have the trial or supervisory experience, that he was a token minority appointment.

Word was that he wouldn't last six months if he got the job, and though he got it and held on tight, those same whispers are still coming from some quarters.

Some lawyers who have left the office describe it as being in a shambles, with lawyers so overworked they are unable to provide decent service.

Taking a shot

One lawyer who left the office after Villareal took over said Villareal has kept his job by tacitly agreeing not to push county supervisors to hire much-needed staff.

The Fresno Bee • Monday, January 9, 1995 B3

is still intolerant of people of color

No such deal, Villareal says. In 1987 the office had 46 lawyers and closed 30,214 cases. Last year it had 55 lawyers and closed 32,389 cases. The number of cases closed per lawyer actually went down by 68 a year.

No simple answers

Villareal warned against drawing overbroad conclusions from the numbers, saying that cases are more complex and time-consuming today. He said there was no question that his lawyers were overworked, but that he had asked for more staff and got it.

A lawyer in Villareal's office, offered the chance to speak confidentially, said he had nothing but good to say about his boss. Lawyer Ralph Avila said Villareal was pleasant to work with, had organized the office better and improved hiring of minorities and women.

"I think he is one of those rare people who brings the office together rather than splitting it

apart," Avila said.

Colleagues in organizations outside the office make similar comments. Mark Miller, a CRLA board member, said Villareal worked well with others and was committed to increasing community input to the legal organization.

In assessing the legal system and other issues, Villareal tends to be blunt. He says he is hopeful that shortcomings can be addressed and that he can be among those making changes.

On courts and minorities: "The court system here is intolerant of people of color. It's bad at best and racist at worst. I'm

not criticizing judges, but a lot of work needs to be done."

On Hispanic progress in the Valley: "It's hard to deal with when you see folks enjoying Mexican culture, eating Mexican food, listening to Mexican music, but you still have this sense that they do not enjoy our company."

Pushing for change

It wasn't too many years ago, he said, that he had to complain about a judge calling Villareal's Hispanic clients "wetbacks" in court.

But Villareal says he will keep pushing for change. He's too stubborn not to.

APPENDIX B

San Jose Magazine Article Regarding the Author

November 1998

The following excerpts are from *The San Jose Magazine* article written **by Dave Clarke** and titled: *Keeper of the Faith: Doing the People's Business; Defender of the Cause.* At the time the author had worked as Santa Clara Public Defender for three years.

"He's a quiet hero," Enriqueta Villarreal says of the man she has stood beside in good times and in bad for 34 years. "People looking at him have no idea what he stands for, what he does." What José Villarreal does is help the helpless, defend the defenseless and protect the meek so one day they might inherit what they've been promised."

"Even the opposition concedes the county and people of Santa Clara have a good one in Villarreal. "There's no question," Santa Clara County District Attorney George Kennedy says, "he's the best Public Defender in the state. From my perspective, sometimes he's a little too successful, but as a citizen, I'm pleased we have as resourceful an advocate as José. He's a gentleman in every sense of the word. He has a broad perspective, he's absolutely committed to his work and he has an excellent understanding of the community."

"He has a certain wisdom," says Susan Bernardini, a supervising attorney in the Public Defender's office. "Some people, particularly lawyers, approach everything they do, well, like lawyers. Not José. He thinks like a human being first, a lawyer second. He knows about life, about people in ways others don't. A client's family may call about their case. Another public defender might analyze whether or not the client's legal needs are being met. If so, that's that, case closed. But José hears the anguish in their voice, he cares about how they feel about their representation, not just whether we met the minimum requirements."

"We had a case where a 76-year-old San José man, feeling threatened and confused discharged a weapon at an unoccupied, illegally-parked vehicle," Bernardini recalls. "The District Attorney sought felony charges and a long prison term against this decorated WWII veteran with a spotless criminal record. Our office eventually got the charges reduced to a misdemeanor with a $100 fine. That's a typical José story. He sees when the system goes awry and grabs it by the shoulders and shakes it. He says **Pay attention! This is a mistake.**"

"Villarreal seems consumed with keeping society as a whole on track. Dropped into this world just across the U.S.-Mexican border, he has proudly, seamlessly melded the two cultures within himself. And while every bit the dreamer of how things might be, Villarreal has his feet planted firmly on the soil he loves. Says Susan Bernardini of her boss's philosophy, "José always tells us, **it's not a perfect world, but make it the best it can be.**"

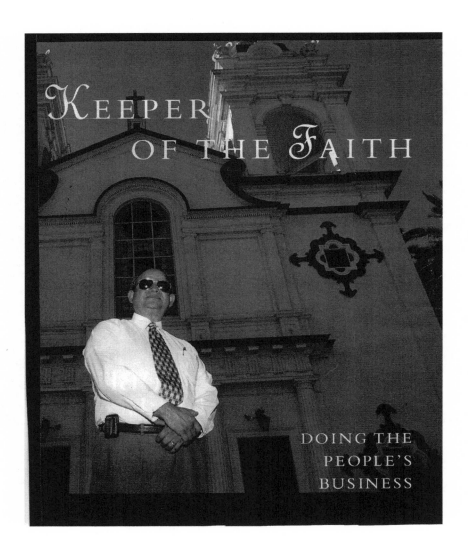

DEFENDER

OF THE

CAUSE

BY DAVE CLARKE

HE'S A QUIET HERO," ENRIQUETA VILLAREAL SAYS OF THE MAN SHE HAS STOOD

beside in good times and bad for 34 years. "People looking at him have no idea what he

stands for, what he does." What Jose Villareal does is help the helpless, defend the de-

fenseless and protect the meek so one day they might

inherit what they've long been promised. In between,

as Santa Clara County's Public Defender, Villareal

makes sure even the soon-to-be-found heinously

guilty are at least afforded the rights they are constitu-

tionally blessed with. ● Even the opposition concedes

the county and people of Santa Clara have a good one

in Villareal. "There's no question," Santa Clara County

District Attorney George Kennedy says, "he's the best

Public Defender in the state. From my perspective, sometimes he's a little too successful,

but as a citizen I'm pleased we have as resourceful an advocate as Jose. He's a gentlemen

in every sense of the word. He has a broad perspective, he's absolutely committed to his

work and he has an excellent understanding of the community."

143

José Rolando Villarreal, J.D.

NDERSTANDING THE COMMUNITY IS SEC-
ond second nature to the man who has been
the county's chief public defender since
1995. Dark, smiling eyes peer out behind
aviator-style wire-framed glasses and the
telltale trace of Chicano inflection can still be heard in his im-
passioned, thoughtful speech. A graduate of James Lick High
School, San Jose State and Santa Clara University Law School,
the man who once labored in central California's fertile fields,
migrating with each new harvest, today oversees a staff of
110 attorneys, 80 support staff and a $22 million budget in an
office that despite all Silicon Valley's affluence, lumbers under a staggering 40,000 cases annually.

"When I first signed on to the public defender's office in
Fresno County, I was only going to be there six months,"
Villareal explains. "I figured I would get a little experience in
trials and litigation, then move on. I was going to be a labor
law specialist, but once I was there I became entrenched in
this idea, this passion for justice. It's cliche, I know, and people
may not believe it, but you get to a point of wanting to do
things for folks not as politically strong or well-represented as
others, those who are otherwise unable to defend themselves.
You just get the idea that you should be there for them."

The county pays its top defender $148,000 annually—a
healthy wage by some standards, but one which pales by comparison to the number most attorneys pencil in on their tax
forms by year's end. "I could leave and do other work. I've
been tempted with lucrative financial offers. My wife wasn't
thrilled when I turned them down, but having been an immigrant, having been poor, a migrant, I found myself making
decisions and choices. This is my choice and I love it."

"He has a certain wisdom," says Susan Bernardini, a supervising attorney in the
Public Defender's of-
fice. "Some people, par-
ticularly lawyers, ap-
proach everything they
do, well, like lawyers.
Not Jose. He thinks like
a human being first, a
lawyer second. He
knows about life, about
people in ways others
don't. A client's family
may call about their
case. Another public de-
fender might analyze
whether or not the
client's legal needs are
being met. If so, that's
that, case closed. But
Jose hears the anguish in
their voice, he cares

County of Santa Clara
OFFICE OF THE
PUBLIC DEFENDER
120 W. MISSION ST.

about how they feel about their representation, not just whether we met the minimum requirements.

"We had a case where a 76-year-old San Jose man, feeling threatened and confused, discharged a weapon at an unoccupied, illegally-parked vehicle," Bernardini recalls. "The District Attorney sought felony charges and a long prison term against this decorated WWII veteran with a spotless criminal record. Our office eventually got the charges reduced to a misdemeanor with a $100 fine. That's a typical Jose story. He sees when the system goes awry and grabs it by the shoulders and shakes it. He says *Pay attention! This is a mistake.*"

verted congregation. But somewhere in the shuffle from *'we're sorry you had a difficult childhood, take a sensitivity training class, please'* to *'three strikes and you're out,'* Villareal believes a fundamental tenet of American justice was lost. "People need to understand what we do and remember why we do it," he says. "We are frequently asked why we represent these people. Everyone wants to get tough on crime, but they seem to forget we still have this basic document called the Constitution, upon which our whole society is based."

"There's a notion," Villareal continues fervently, "that our job is keeping criminals out of jail, that our clients are not hu-

"People need to understand what we do and remember why we do it. Everyone wants to get tough on crime, but they seem to forget we still have this basic document called the Constitution upon which our whole society is based."

There is a connection between Villareal and this place, this soil, these people.

As a young man, Villareal picking grapes in Pleasanton (L.)

After years in which citizens were assaulted by criminals then victimized by a legal system that imposed little more than a slap on the wrist against perpetrators, the pendulum has swung back toward stiffer sentences. Law enforcement agencies and public officials on both sides of the legislative aisle preach tough-on-crime sentiments to an already-con-

man. But the process they go through is dehumanizing. It takes away human dignity. People have to understand who our clients are. They are parents, they are children, they are taxpayers. They are *us,*" he rails vigilantly. "This constant barrage of *'Put them away forever'* gets out of control. When you see sentences of a hundred years, two, three hundred years, it reflects a society that is vindictive, rather than sensitive to human beings in difficult situations. Sometimes, the circumstances prove a person just happens to be in the wrong place at the wrong time."

By most everyone's measure, Villareal is generous, with a warm, giving heart, but he also has what it takes to get the job done. "Being an administrator is tough," notes Bernardini. "You have to say *No.* You have to fire people. Jose doesn't just shine it on or pass it off onto someone else. He takes input on things. And once he's come to a decision, he sticks with it. Others before him were intimidated and wishy-washy. He takes care of business."

José Rolando Villarreal, J.D.

Villareal not only 'takes care of business' on the job, but at home and in the community too. Honored as Citizen of the Year by the Latino Peace Officers Association in 1988 and Lawyer of the Year by Fresno County's La Raza Lawyers' Association, he also received the coveted Cruz Reynoso Community Services Award from the California La Raza Lawyers' Association. Add to that his membership on the boards of the Mexican Heritage Corporation of San Jose and the Metropolitan YMCA, his appointment to the California Commission on Access to Justice and his involve-

The fruits of their labor: the Villareal family. (L-R) Rolando, Alejandro, Meliza and Adrian.

ment with Evergreen Valley Community College's EN-LACE Program and you wonder where he finds the time. "People always ask how he does it," Enriqueta Villareal says. "He just does."

And if helping everyone else's children find their way in a complex world weren't enough, Villareal still found time for his own four children. "He was always there in the stands for our kids' games in school," his wife remembers.

"They weren't superstars, but he never missed a game. Six months before our youngest was to graduate from high school in Fresno, Jose was offered the alternate public defender's job in San Diego county. He asked me what I thought he should do. I told him to accept the offer. He could come back on weekends, we could go down there. It was only a few months, we would be OK. In the end, he decided he couldn't miss his son's games, however few remained. He turned down the position and we waited for the season to end."

FAMILY AND CHILDREN, ESPECIALLY, ARE OF paramount importance to Villareal. "I had a case in Fresno county," he explains, "where the court wanted to incarcerate a thirteen-year-old child for not going to school. Other than not wanting to, there are usually reasons why a child doesn't go to school. This young man was unable to read, he was humiliated when he read in front of the class and it wasn't really his fault. I appealed his case, which is something we as public defenders rarely do, this time all the way to State Supreme Court. Although I lost the case, it was very satisfying nonetheless. From my challenge, a process was established which local courts must follow before detaining a juvenile for not going to school. Is that a big issue?" Villareal asks. "At a time when the dividing line between child and adult gets more blurry with each passing day, it becomes extremely significant. It became part of the recipe that children should be given every opportunity to be educated, not incarcerated. Only recently have we begun to get into prevention and education, to take a systemwide approach. Only now are we placing responsibility on the school system, on the parents, on other segments of society rather than solely on the child. For me, this was a very important case."

Villareal's office represents thousands of children. Most of them, he says, are followers. "We need to understand their circumstances. There are enormous pressures on kids today. In many cases, it's the parents who should be in jail, not the children. We push these kids up against the wall, then when they react we punish them for reacting. This should not be acceptable to us. We need to care more for our kids, be more involved. If not, we fail as a society."

Villareal seems consumed with keeping society as a whole on track. Dropped into this world just across the U.S.-Mexican border, he has proudly, seamlessly melded the two cultures within himself. And while every bit the dreamer of how things might be, Villareal has his feet planted firmly on the soil he loves. Says Susan Bernardini of her boss' philosophy, "Jose always tells us, *It's not a perfect world, but make it the best it can be.*" ⬛

> If helping everyone else's children
>
> find their way in a complex
>
> world weren't enough,
>
> Villareal still found time
>
> for his own four children.

APPENDIX C

Additional Photographs

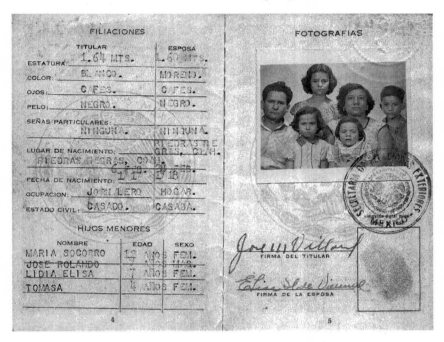

October 1953 Legal Document for Permanent Residency in the USA

Eleven years later, December 1964, my parents' 25th anniversary celebration

Spanish Church with the attached convent on the right at the Plaza de Tres Culturas

*By 1947, the convent had been converted to the aduana
(The Federal Customs Building).*

I was visiting Parque Chapultepec in 1947, while living in Mexico City.

After searching for this building on several visits to Mexico City, I finally found the aduana on our last trip in 2017. I felt goosebumps all over as I walked into the patio of the building where I lived and played as a two and a half-year old.

San Jose State University graduation day with my son and daughter before leaving our house to the graduation ceremony, June 1968.

SJSU 1968 graduation celebration with my grandmother, Concepcion Torres Heredia, who came from Piedras Negras specifically for the graduation.

Playing with my daughter as I took a break from my studies - 1968.

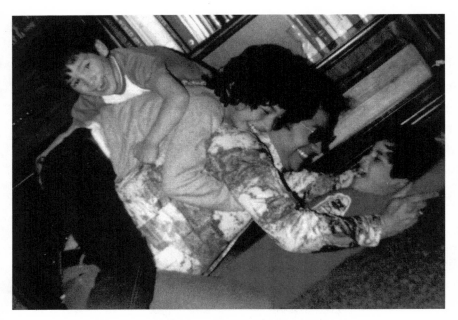

Playing with my three sons, an after-work ritual-1975

My mother and I at Mi Tierra Cafe, Market Place Entrance

(left to right) Mr. Jorge Cortez (son of original owner of Mi Tierra) and myself. Mi Tierra Café and Bakery, Market Place Entrance

BIBLIOGRAPHY

Acuña, Rodolfo. 1972. *Occupied America: A History of Chicanos*. Harper Collins Publishers

Arreola, Daniel D. 2002. *Tejano South Texas: A Mexican American Cultural Province*. University of Texas Press.

Arreola, James R. 1993. *The Mexican Border Cities: Landscape Anatomy and Place Personality*. University of Arizona Press.

Arellano, Gustavo. 2007. *Ask a Mexican*. Simon & Schuster

Aguayo, Rafael. 1990. *Dr. Deming: the American Who Taught the Japanese About Quality*. Fireside.

Baker, Daniel B. 1992. *Power Quotes*. Visible Ink Press

Bennis, Warren. 1989. *On Becoming a Leader*. Perseus Books Group.

Camarrillo, Albert. 1979. *Chicanos in a Changing Society: From Mexican Pueblos to American Barrios in Santa Barbara and Southern California, 1848-1930*. Cambridge: Harvard University Press.

Chopra, Deepak. 2010. *The Soul of Leadership: Unlocking Your Potential For Greatness*. Random House Inc.

Castañeda, Jorge. 2007. *Ex Mex: From Migrants to Immigrants*. The New Press.

Caissy, Gail. 1998. *Unlock the Fear: How to open Yourself up to Face and Accept Change*. Insight Books. Plenum Publishing Corporation.

De León, Arnoldo. 1983. *They Called Them Greasers: Anglo Attitudes Toward Mexicans in Texas, 1821-1900*. Austin: University of Texas Press.

Daniels, Roger. 1972. *Racism in California: A Reader in the History of Oppression*. The Macmillan Company.

Eisenhower, John S. D. 1993. *Intervention*. W.W. Norton & Company.

Ellis, Joseph J. 2001. *The Founding Brothers: The Revolutionary Generation*. Random House Inc.

Ellis, Joseph J. 2007. *American Creation: Triumphs and Tragedies at the Founding of the Republic*. Random House Inc.

De Mente, Boye. 1996. *NTC's Dictionary of Mexican Cultural Code Words: The Complete Guide to Key Words that Express how the Mexicans Think, Communicate, and Behave.* NTC Publishing Group.

Fulton, Roger. 1995. *Common Sense Leadership: Handbook for Success as A Leader.* Barnes & Noble Books.

Fox, Geoffrey. 1996. *Hispanic Nation: Culture, Politics, and the Constructing of Identity.* The University of Arizona Press.

Gardner, John W. 1990. *On Leadership.* Free Press, New York.

Giber, David. 2000. *Best Practices in Leadership Development Handbook.* Jossey-Bass/Pfeiffer.

Goodwin, Doris Kearns. 2018. *Leadership in Turbulent Times.* Simon & Schuster.

Gutiérrez, José Angel. 1998. *The Making of a Chicano Militant: Lessons from Cristal.* The University of Wisconsin Press.

Gutiérrez, José Angel. 2003. *A Chicano Manual on How to Handle Gringos.* Arte Public Press.

Gutiérrez-Jones, Carl. 1995. *Rethinking the Borderlands: Between Culture and the Legal Discourse.* University of California.

Hanson, Victor Davis, 2003. *Mexifornia: A State of Becoming.* Encounter Books.

Hayner, Don and McNamee, Tom. 1988. *Streetwise Chicago.* Loyola University Press.

Heifetz, Ronald A. 1994. *Leadership without Easy Answers.* The Belknap Press of Harvard University.

Hernandez, Kelly Lytle. 2010. *Migra! A History of the U.S. Border Patrol.* University of California Press.

Kandell, Jonathan. 1988. *La Capital: The Biography of Mexico City.* Random House New York.

Kennedy, Edward M. 2006. *America: Back on Track.* Penguin Group.

Leavitt, Ronnie. 2010. *Cultural Competence: A Lifelong Journey to Cultural Proficiency.* SLAK Incorporated.

LeBaron, Michelle. 2003. *Bridging Cultural Conflicts: A New Approach for a Changing World.* Jossey-Bass.

Maharidge, Dale. 1996. *The Coming White Minority: California's Eruptions and the Nation's Future.* Times Books Random House.

Maxwell, John C. 2000. *Failing Forward: Turning Mistakes into Stepping Stones for Success*. Thomas Nelson, Inc.

Maxwell, John C. 2002. *Leadership 101: What Every Leader Needs to Know*. Thomas Nelson, Inc.

McCullough, David. 2017. *The American Spirit*. Simon & Schuster.

McWilliams, Carey. 1990. *North from Mexico*. Praeger Publishers.

Montoya, Maceo. 2016. *Chicano Movement for Beginners*. For Beginners LLC.

Morales, Ed. 2003. *Living in Spanglish: The Search for Latino Identity in America*. St. Martini's Press.

Mirandé, Alfredo. 1987. *Gringo Justice*. University of Notre Dame Press.

Mirandé, Alfredo. 1985. *The Chicano Experience: An Alternative Perspective*. University of Notre Dame Press.

Miller, Tom. 1981. *On the Border: Portraits of America's Southwestern Frontier*. The University of Arizona Press.

Montejano, David. 1987. *Anglos and Mexicans in the Making of Texas, 1836-1986*. Austin: University of Texas Press.

Moore, Joan. 1993. *In the Barrio: Latinos and the Underclass Debate*. Russell Sage Foundation.

Moore, Joanne I. 1999. *Immigrants in Court*. University of Washington Press.

Muñoz, Carlos Jr. 1989. *Youth, Identity, Power: The Chicano Movement*. Verso.

Nair, Keshavan. 1994. *A Higher Standard of Leadership: Lessons from The Life of Gandhi*. Berrett-Koehler Publishers.

Nesmith, Samuel P. 1981. *Our Mexican Ancestors*. University of Texas Institute of Texan Cultures at San Antonio.

Noona Guerra, Mary Ann. 1988. *The History of San Antonio's Market Square*. The Alamo Press

O'Neil, Tip. 1994. *All Politics is Local*. Times Books.

Ortega, Mariano. 2017. *To Be or Not to Be: A Map of Human Behavior*. Fomeq.

Paulett, John and Gordon, Ron. 2004. *Forgotten Chicago*. Arcadia Publishing.

Poniatowska, Elena. 2014. *La Noche de Tlatelolco*. Ediciones Era. S.A. de C.V.

Posner, Barry and Kouzes, James M. 1987. *The Leadership Challenge: How to get Extraordinary Things Done in Organizations*. Jossey-Bass Inc.

Regua, Nannette and Villarreal, Arturo. 2009. *Mexicans in San José: Images of America*. Arcadia Publishing.

Riding, Alan. 1984. *Distant Neighbors; A Portrait of the Mexicans.* Random House.

Rodriguez, Gloria G., Ph.D. 1999. *Raising Nuestros Niños: Bringing up Latino Children in a Bicultural World.* Fireside Books.

Romo, Ricardo. 1983. *East Los Angeles: History of a Barrio.* University of Texas Press.

Ruiz, Miguel. 1997. *The Four Agreements: A Practical Guide to Personal Freedom.* Amber-Allen Publishing.

Sanchez, George J. 1993. *Becoming Mexican: Ethnicity, Culture, and Identity in Chicano Los Angeles, 1900-1945.* Oxford University Press.

St. Onge, Patricia. 2009. *Embracing Cultural Competency: A Roadmap for Non-Profit Capacity Builders.* Fieldstone Alliance.

Toricelli, Robert G. 2001. *Quotations for Public Speakers.* Rutgers University Press.

Turner, Robyn. 1996. *Texas Traditions: The Culture of The Lone Star.* Little, Brown, and Company.

Villarreal, José Antonio. 1959. *Pocho.* Anchor Books.

Villarreal Martinez, Rafael. 2010. *Piedras Negras, Destino y Origen: Personajes, Sitios y Recuerdos.* ISBN. Impreso en Mexico.

Villaseñor, Victor. 1991. *Rain of Gold.* Dell Publishing.

Weeks, Dudley, Ph.D. 1992. *The Eight Essential Steps to Conflict Resolution.* G.P. Putnam's Sons.

White, B. Joseph. 2010. *La Naturaleza del Liderazgo: Reptiles, Mamíferos y el Reto de Convertirse en un Gran Líder.* Grupo Nelson, Inc.

Wood, Andrew Grant. 2001. *On the Border: Society and Culture Between United States and Mexico.* SR Books.

Zamora, Emilio and Orozco, Cynthia. 2000. *Mexican Americans in Texas History: Selected Essays.* Texas State Historical Association.